proclamation 2

Aids for Interpreting the Lessons of the Church Year

Elisabeth Schüssler Fiorenza
and
† Urban T. Holmes

series b

editors: Elizabeth Achtemeier · Gerhard Krodel · Charles P. Price

FORTRESS PRESS PHILADELPHIA

Library of Congress Cataloging in Publication Data (Revised)
Main entry under title:

Proclamation 2.

Consists of 24 volumes in 3 series designated A, B, and C which correspond to the cycles of the three year lectionary plus 4 volumes covering the lesser festivals. Each series contains 8 basic volumes with the following titles: Advent-Christmas, Epiphany, Lent, Holy Week, Easter, Pentecost 1, Pentecost 2, and Pentecost 3.
CONTENTS: [etc.]—Series C: [1] Fuller, R. H. Advent-Christmas. [2] Pervo, R. I. and Carl III, W. J. Epiphany.—Thulin, R. L. et al. The lesser festivals. 4 v.
1. Bible—Homiletical use. 2. Bible—Liturgical lessons, English.
[BS534.5.P76] 251 79–7377
ISBN 0–8006–4079–9 (ser. C, v. 1)

9011G81 Printed in the United States of America 1–4070

Contents

Editor's Foreword

The season of Lent has an interesting history. Some have thought that it grew out of the first-century church's customary practice of fasting the day before Easter. Certainly by the end of the second century the devout voluntarily extended that fast to two or seven or fourteen days. However, that fast foreshadowed the fast of Holy Week and was not the source of the Lenten practice of fasting. Rather, the latter came from the special disciplines imposed upon catechumens during the final stage of their preparation for baptism at the Easter vigil.

New converts were received into the early church during the paschal vigil, which was held from Saturday evening to Easter dawn. In the ceremony of the vigil, a lamp was lit and blessed, lessons were read, the bishop preached, and finally the neophytes were baptized and confirmed into the body of Christ, after which they joined the faithful in intercessory prayers and the Eucharist.

Prior to such entrance into the church, converts underwent three weeks of catechesis, or fasting and instruction in Christian doctrine. Under the influence of the monastic-ascetic movement, it became the custom for all of the faithful to join the catechumens in these exercises. Thus the disciplines of Lent were born.

The extension of the observance to a longer period apparently took place during the fourth century. The Jerusalem church historicized the liturgy by turning the various festivals into commemorations of events in the life of Jesus. The time of Lent, therefore, came to be identified with Jesus' forty days in the wilderness. But the forty days were calculated in different ways in different churches. Neither Saturday nor Sunday was a fast day, so sometimes the forty days spread over eight or nine weeks before Easter. It was Rome which established, by the seventh century, the length of the season as we now know it.

The ceremony of placing ashes on the forehead—from which Ash Wednesday takes its name—probably originated in Gaul in the sixth century. At first the ceremony was confined to those guilty of grave sins who were doing public penance for their offenses, but the practice gradually spread throughout the church as a form of penance for all.

After the church was accepted by the state in the fourth century, Lent took on new importance as the time when Christians separated themselves from worldly ways and submitted to the yoke of Christ. Early Lenten preaching strongly insisted on mutual forgiveness and forbearance among church members, intensification of private prayer, generosity in giving, regular attendance at biblical and doctrinal instruction, and strict physical abstention from food. Such disciplines were obligatory for all church members no matter what their status or spiritual state. The acceptance of Lenten disciplines reminded both the careless Christian and the devout of the claims of the Christian standard: "Do not be conformed to this world but be transformed by the renewal of your mind . . ." (Rom. 12:2). The disciplines of Lent can function in the same manner today.

Our exegete for this volume is Dr. Elisabeth Schüssler Fiorenza, Professor of Theology and New Testament Studies at the University of Notre Dame. Dr. Fiorenza is author of *The Apocalypse, Invitation to Revelation, Revelation* in the Proclamation Commentaries series, and two books in German. She has served as an editor for Roman Catholic and Protestant publications and is widely known for her contributions to both scholarship and the women's movement. She has been assisted by Mr. Fred Holper, who has made some stylistic corrections in her manuscript.

The homiletician for this volume, the Very Rev. Urban T. Holmes, III, died unexpectedly after completing this project. He was dean of the School of Theology, University of the South, and earlier in his life had had wide experience in both parish and university settings. He was a graduate of the Philadelphia Divinity School, the University of the South, and Marquette University (Ph.D. in Theology and Society). Dr. Holmes was the author of seven books, co-author and editor of five others, and Director of the *Anglican Theological Review*. Most recently he had published *Praying with the Family of God* and *The Priest in Community*. His contributions to his own church body, the Episcopal Church, were enhanced by a deep ecumenical commitment. He is remembered by his wife, four children, and countless friends. It is fitting that this small book, *Lent,* be thankfully dedicated to his memory.

ELIZABETH ACHTEMEIER

Ash Wednesday

Lutheran	Roman Catholic	Episcopal	Pres/UCC/Chr	Meth/COCU
Joel 2:12–19	Joel 2:12–18	Joel 2:1–2, 12–17 or Isa. 58:1–12	Isa. 58:3–12	Isa. 58:1–12
2 Cor. 5:20b–6:2	2 Cor. 5:20–6:2	2 Cor. 5:20b–6:10	James 1:12–18	James 1:12–18
Matt. 6:1–6, 16–21	Matt. 6:1–6, 16–18	Matt. 6:1–6, 16–21	Mark 2:15–20	Mark 2:15–20

EXEGESIS

First Lesson: Isa. 58:1–12. The readings for Lent begin with Trito-Isaiah's exhortation to undergo a "true fast" genuinely pleasing to God. Isa. 58:1–12 is best understood as an exhortation composed of different prophetic forms. V. 3a asks for the true and effective way of fasting. The response in v. 5 asks, "Is your way of fasting pleasing to God?" The answer is "No." A fast pleasing to God is spelled out in vv. 6–7. Vv. 8–9a and 10b–11 contain a promise of salvation; they refer to God in the third person, and—except for v. 12—they address the individual, not the people of Israel. While the whole section begins with a prophetic word of exhortation similar to traditional prophetic oracles (cf. Hos. 8:1; Mic. 3:8), it concludes with a conditional announcement of blessing and salvation similar to Trito-Isaiah 60—62 and Job 11:13–19. Thus, this pericope is a postexilic composition which, in the tradition of the classical prophets, insists upon the doing of justice as the concomitant expression of a true fast. The theological problem of a proper fast is typical of the postexilic community (cf. Zech. 7:3; 8:19).

The introduction in v. 1 emphasizes that what follows is spoken with divine authorization and power (cf. 61:1–2). The prophet here speaks to a community assembly gathered for a liturgy of fasting. While the Law prescribed a fast only on the Day of Atonement (cf. Lev. 23:26ff.), Israel in later times came to observe other fasts with liturgical signs of mortification and mourning. Such fasts commemorated fateful calamities that had chastened the nation (for example, the destruction of the temple), begged for God's mercy in the face of disaster (cf. Joel 2:12–19), or expressed private penance and contrition.

In contrast to the preexilic prophetic oracles of judgment and chastisement, the prophet here (vv. 2–3a) concedes that Israel is seeking to please Yahweh, to know and do the will of God, and to delight in approaching God in the liturgy. But God pays no attention to their fast and mortification. Vv. 3b–4 explain why God fails to hear their cries for help. Like Amos (2:8), Trito-Isaiah stresses that the liturgy of fasting is made worthless because of continued injustice. The people exploit their workers, fight and compete in business dealings, and fail even to shy away from actual violence.

V. 5 provides a somewhat different interpretation of the proper fast. Ironically, it criticizes external liturgical rites and behavior. Such outward behavior does not indicate a "fast acceptable to God." By contrast, vv. 6–7 outline behavior which is acceptable as genuine fasting. It is not that the Israelites should do works of social justice instead of fasting, but rather that the practice of social liberation and justice constitutes the acceptable fast.

Liberation from every yoke of slavery and the sharing of food with the hungry are more pleasing to God than rites of mortification and fasting. Human liberation is thus more important than any cultic rites appealing directly to God.

Vv. 8–12, through new words and images of salvation, elaborate upon the future blessings which will accrue to the individual and nation if and when they cease to pervert justice and begin to feed the hungry and liberate the oppressed. Then God will answer their fast. Then they will grow healthy and strong, famous and wealthy. Then their light will "rise like dawn out of darkness." Then God will guide the individual and the nation and rebuild their ruins and cities. Then, finally, God will hear their prayer and respond: "Here I am." God's presence has as an unconditional premise the social justice and liberation praxis of the people of God.

Second Lesson: James 1:12–18. Though the content and major theme of this passage are rather clear, the argument's literary structure and concrete expression are not. Theologically, the passage seeks to make clear that temptations do not originate with God.

This section begins with a makarism, or beatitude, which refers back to the theme of 1:2–4. Here, however, the address is to the individual person and not to the whole community. The beatitude shows its apocalyptic character when it speaks of steadfast endurance in the face of the eschatological trial, and of eschatological salvation. Like Rev. 2:10, the beatitude promises the victory crown of eternal life to the one who overcomes the eschatological trial. God promises glorious salvation to those "who love God." This formula is found frequently in early Christian literature (cf. 1 Cor. 2:9; Rom. 8:28; Eph. 6:24; 1 Clem. 34:8). People who love God must endure eschatological affliction. Thus, the whole beatitude appears to reflect traditional apocalyptic theology.

In vv. 13–18 the beatitude is reinterpreted in a moral-anthropological sense. The reinterpretation is expressed, however, in mythological-metaphorical language whose historical-religious context is Jewish-Hellenistic wisdom theology. Although *Sophia* Wisdom is not explicitly mentioned here, we do find a similar juxtaposition in 3:13–18, where there is a contrast between the wisdom that "comes not from above" and the Wisdom from above. Similarly, 1:16 states that "every good and perfect gift comes from above."

V. 13 insists that we cannot blame God for temptations which overcome us. Since God cannot be tempted by evil, it follows that God does not tempt anyone either. V. 17a makes the same point in a positive way in the form of a hexameter (cf. 1 Cor. 15:33). Every good comes from God—here called the "Father of Stars"—who is without change, solstice, or eclipse. Not a trace of that change which determines the cosmic order is to be found in God (17b). God, who is the origin of all good and well-being, is incapable of effecting evil since such a change would be contrary to God's very nature. The stars and other heavenly bodies may herald change, but God, who is their creator, is above change.

Vv. 14f. and 18 draw out this contrast in the language of mythological personification and a metaphor of birth. Human desire is personified as a female who lures and entices each person into temptation. When Desire has conceived, she gives birth to sin, which then matures and in turn gives birth to death. The concatenation is a rhetorical device elaborating the "birthing" process and tradition (v. 15). Using the same imagery, v. 18 characterizes God as a woman who gives birth. Exegetes hasten to explain this female language as metaphorical language but fail to realize that all God-language is metaphorical. God, according to his eternal will, "gives birth" to Christians who become, in effect, the downpayment, the firstborn of the new creation.

Christians understand themselves as reborn to herald the eschatological new creation. Thus, the first creation is expressed through the metaphor of paternity, but the "new" creation is described in maternal imagery. This is possible because, in early Christian wisdom theology, Divine Wisdom and the Holy Spirit—as well as the gospel—were closely associated.

Gospel: Mark 2:15–20. This Gospel unites parts of two controversy dialogues: one concerning Jesus' table community with tax collectors and sinners (2:13–17), and the other concerning the question of fasting (2:18–22). Both controversy dialogues probably were brought together by Christian communities in Galilee or Syria in the middle of the first century. Mark places these conflict stories in Capernaum and introduces them with an interpretive headline in 2:2: Jesus teaches the word (*ton logon*). The expression, "the word," in the absolute is found elsewhere in the interpretation of the Parable of the Sower (Mark 4:14). For Mark, then, 2:1—3:6 is a summary of the content of Jesus' teachings. These teachings fly in the face of the Pharisaic observance of the Torah. Therefore it is understandable that his opponents would make plans to kill him. Like the pre-Markan controversy collection, Mark stresses that Jesus' preaching led to his execution. The Gospel, therefore, announces this connection at the very beginning of Jesus' public ministry.

The first controversy dialogue of our reading is introduced by a story about the call of the tax collector Levi. This story is a formal parallel to the call of the first disciples in 1:16–20. Levi is a paradigmatic example of the tax collectors who share the table community of Jesus and the later church. The additional remark in v. 15c that "there were many who followed him" (the Greek implies a continuous, not yet concluded action) emphasizes that in the time of the church, discipleship was expressed through table community with the Lord. Jesus is portrayed as head of a house-church (in his house) who celebrates eucharistic table community with those who, according to Jewish law, were the outcasts of both society and religion. Since the story reflects very old traditions about Jesus' actual behavior (cf. Luke 7:34 par. Matt. 11:19, a Q saying; Luke 15:1), the church in Galilee which probably formulated this story was using the example of Jesus to justify its practice of table community with persons who were suspect and disreputable.

The story climaxes with two sayings in v. 17. The first saying was a favorite metaphor of the itinerant Hellenistic philosophers. When they were reproached for associating with lower-class people, they would reply that physicians do not usually teach among the healthy but among those who are sick. The church, in formulating this story, summed up Jesus' activity by using this very popular metaphor. The second saying emphasizes that Jesus did not come to call the righteous, the pious, and the orthodox, but those who heard his call and were prepared to follow him, especially the outcasts and sinners. It is significant that, unlike Luke, Mark does not add "to repentance." In pre-Markan as well as Markan theology, not repentance but discipleship and table community are constituents of the church.

In the second conflict story the focus is upon fasting, and the emphasis has shifted from Jesus to the disciples. Whereas in the Q saying of Luke 7:33ff. Jesus' nonascetic practice is contrasted with the asceticism of John the Baptist, here the practice of the disciples is contrasted with that of the disciples of John and the Pharisees. Two contradictory answers are given to this accusation. The first reply, in vv. 21–22 (which was not, significantly, included in this reading), stresses that the disciples do not fast because there is no compromise possible between the old and new life styles. The second response, in vv. 19b–20, seems to have been inserted at a later stage of the tradition when the church had reintroduced fasting and ascetic practices (cf. Acts 13:2; 14:23; Didache 8:1). This response serves as theological justification for the fact that Christians had begun to observe fasting again. It does so by emphasizing that Christians fast because they do not yet share in the eschatological table community and salvation. These two controversy dialogues, therefore, appear to apply what was said about Jesus in the Q tradition to the Christian community: he was accused, on one hand, of being a "glutton and drunkard" for not fasting as John the Baptist had and, on the other hand, of "being a friend of tax collectors and sinners."

HOMILETICAL INTERPRETATION

First Lesson: Isa. 58:1–12. The church occasionally reads a seemingly contradictory pericope on Ash Wednesday, one of the two most solemn fast days in her calendar (the other being Good Friday). This one would appear to dismiss the value of fasting save in the most equivocal sense. The act of freeing the oppressed, on the one hand, can only be called an oblique metaphor for "fasting." Much of the behavior which the author of this passage condemns with cutting sarcasm, on the other hand, is precisely what will go on in many of the churches in some of the denominations that will read this passage. We will "bow our heads like a bulrush," and "make our bed on sackcloth and ashes"—or the liturgical equivalent.

Are we to change our liturgies? Are we to feel guilty about what we do? Such questions miss the point of the prophetic challenge. We need to keep in mind that the OT phenomenon of prophecy arose out of the

Hebrew and Jewish cult, not, as we sometimes think, in opposition to it. Whereas the relation of this passage to what precedes it from Isa. 40 on is in dispute—there are those who question the existence of a Trito-Isaiah, and certainly the date of this passage is debatable—it appears probable that these words were uttered at a time in which the Jews were involved in restoring the temple at Jerusalem. The author was a contemporary of some of the Priestly writers. Both the temple and the Priestly code are concerned for Jewish ritual law, including fasting.

Can we justify this concern for religious observance? Cult or liturgy, and spiritual exercises such as fasting are very much concerned with the formation of the person. Religion is more than a commitment to moral action. It concerns the transformation of the whole person. Christianity has no corner on an abhorrence of hunger, injustice, and oppression. What distinguishes us is our identification with the mind of Christ at a deeper level than ideology. We are called to be transformed by the indwelling of Christ. We are shaped through discipleship to him at the level of our deepest selves. The practice of religion in liturgy and spiritual exercises, when understood, seeks to effect a formation that is consistent at every level of the person.

It is not a question of either/or. The author of this passage is undoubtedly quite correct when he describes persons who fast in the name of God and yet countenance or even participate in oppression. How many of us who lament our sins on Ash Wednesday have participated in industrial practices which, in the name of profit, arbitrarily deprive people of a livelihood, or have done nothing to protest genocide in South Africa? Ascetic practice which does not issue in action is more than just suspect; it is immoral.

But going about "doing good" with no vision of what that action is to effect in a relation to God is equally wrong. It is like a marriage where we never set aside our own agenda in order that we may be open to the will of our spouse. Good listening precedes good action. Fasting is an activity which may in fact help us listen.

One is reminded of the delightful story told of the pastor who preached on the parable of the Pharisee and the tax gatherer (Luke 18:9–14). At the end of his sermon the pastor began his prayer: "Lord, we thank thee that we are not as that Pharisee. . . ." The Pharisees were very good people, the best of their day, and they fasted, which is one reason why they were very good people. The problem was that fasting which becomes an end in itself is not enough.

The Ash Wednesday fast is an act of spiritual discipline in accord with the best of Christian practice. It is a concrete exercise in putting God before mammon. The intention is to make our lives more simple, more pure in heart, so that we may see the vision of God for his creation and act. Fasting can sensitize us. Fasting is one way to shape our consciousness in more than an abstract, disembodied manner. I imagine that the author of this passage fasted regularly. This is what enabled him to see the contradiction between being pious and yet failing to do anything about the suffering of humanity.

Let us not be as foolish as those in the sixties who announced that they had grown beyond religious practice, and whose "piety" consisted of prophetic witness—they had no staying power. Their orientation was as different from that of Isaiah as Platonic love and a passion that pulls at our guts. The people who really change our society, people like Martin Luther King, Jr., more likely than not know what it means to fast.

Second Lesson: James 1:12–18. This passage is loaded with some profound theological questions. It begins by saying endurance has a payoff: the gift of life. This notion has been honored more in its abuse than not. As the exegesis points out, the beatitude (which is a common Jewish rhetorical device) refers back to vv. 2–3, which suggest that we should be happy when everything is going badly, because then we can acquire the virtue of fortitude—a trait most desirable for Christians. This "pop Stoicism" (at the time this letter was written, it was the prevailing philosophy and was mixed with a smattering of Platonism and a dash of Neo-Pythagoreanism) lies behind the worst in Pollyanna, on the one hand, and in the dourness of Thomas Hardy, on the other hand.

Yet when we think about it, the author is calling for courage, a discipline born of a consistent spirituality, something that says a great deal more profound to us than simply "celebrate life." Simone Weil's collection of essays entitled *Waiting for God* draws the term "waiting" from the Greek *hupomenei,* the same Greek verb as in v. 12, where it is translated "endures" or "remains steadfast." Weil, who was a Jewish convert to Roman Catholicism and a French resistance fighter during World War II, made the point that the person who would know God must "wait" upon him, must "remain steadfast." As she said, we have to enter into affliction, and only when we have done so will the gift of life be given. Weil was no grim Pietist. She tells us that one of the three experiences that were instrumental in her conversion was her discovery of George Herbert's (1594–1633) sensitive and delightful poem, "Love bade me welcome." It describes a God who beguiles us into dining with him.

The author of James assures us that temptation does not come from

God. If not, where does it come from? He answers that with an equation typical of his times: lust creates temptation, which leads to sin. Lust is inordinate desire, of which sexual appetite is only a very familiar example. James's explanation really solves little. If lust is a part of our natural being, what is the source of its corruption? If it is a part of ourselves (that is, the body) in which the soul is imprisoned, who created that part if God did not? Elsewhere in the Bible, particularly in Job, God does indeed tempt us, but this is obviously contrary to the author's doctrine of God.

The God described here is a very Greek God. He is pure light, he does not change, he is without emotions, and he is devoid of shadows. He is utterly simple—an unmixed substance. The preacher has to deal with this passage and decide what to do about that kind of description of God. It does not accord with what we are told of God elsewhere in the Scriptures, although it is unimpeachably orthodox. It is this doctrine of God, however, which leads to the impasse found in the author's attempts to explain the source of temptation as lying in our own lusts or inordinate desires.

Process theology has attempted to suggest that God does change, because creation is a part of him (pantheism), and inasmuch as creation is not complete, neither is God. God is, in this sense, both absolute and consequent. This is a more dynamic notion of God than the very static one offered in James. Temptation arises from the incompleteness of creation, and in a sense pertains to God.

C. G. Jung argues that humanity is made in the image of God and includes that shadow or dark side which is repressed or left undifferentiated in the process of the differentiation of the ego into an integrated, conscious self. Jung insisted that God does have a shadow, which, like everyone else's shadow, is not the same thing as evil but is a source of temptation that can lead to evil.

This is related to Thomas Merton's claim that spiritual growth requires the experience of dread, which is the confrontation with the coincidence of good and evil as we seek union with God. Again this is a more dynamic explanation of temptation than the one the author of James provides.

There is a cosmic dimension to temptation which gets us beyond an overweaning, pedantic concern for lust, one to which we would do well to attend. If we are going to make more of "remaining steadfast" than a Stoic resistance to several temptations, it will come about only as we have a wider view of the source of temptation.

Gospel: Mark 2:15–20. This passage is a redaction made by the early Christian community, which apparently fasted; so let us move beyond the argument of whether or not to fast, which we discussed under the Old Testament lesson. At issue here is the meaning of confrontation with a Jesus who offends our sensibilities about what is proper. He ate with sinners. While others took the ritual law very seriously, he seemed to be enjoying the good life.

Why would such behavior lead to his crucifixion? Obviously there is a profound threat in what he did. Mary Douglas, an anthropologist, has a theory that the Jewish dietary laws are derived from the need to control the environment. She points out that what threatens people are those things which do not fit their categories (for example, an animal with a cloven hoof, the pig that does not chew its cud as do cattle). The rule of not eating with bad people relates to the fact that a shared meal is a relatively intimate form of social intercourse, and we must not run the risk of being "infected" by their sin.

The rabbis taught that cleanliness was next to godliness. Puritanism in every age concurs. G. K. Chesterton's observation was that the saint can afford to be filthy: it is only required of seducers that they be clean.

What Jesus threatened was the structures by which people organized their lives in order to protect themselves from those things that they could not control. I recall a pastoral relationship with a family in which a young person was expelled from school for selling several marijuana cigarettes. All evidence was that she was immature for her age, but that she was not a habitual user or a hardened "pusher." But it was impossible to get her into another school. The only conclusion we could draw was that she was to be sacrificed in order to protect others from her "disease." It was an issue of control.

The threat of Jesus was that he embodied what moralizers fear most. To quote Dorothy Sayers, the English novelist and playwright, he did not "fit." This was Jesus' power as well as his threat. He was a scandal, a stone that caused people to stumble over their own neat categories. Jesus courted chaos by challenging neat presuppositions.

Chaos is the name we give to unstructured or undifferentiated existence. Our fear of chaos is the flip side of our need to name our experience, to make sense out of our existence. Chaos is the source of creativity and growth. But when chaos appears about to overwhelm us, we are all too ready to quiet our fears by ordering what little of life we can and shutting out the rest. Jesus clearly challenged this tendency in the people of his day as he preached repentance—that is, a new way of seeing things—as a precondition for the breaking-in of the Kingdom of God.

Ash Wednesday is the first day of Lent. One way of looking at the next forty days is as an opportunity to lay aside our need for control and to enter into the chaos of our inner selves, our society, and the world. This is quite different from the usual spirit of Lent, which is to "tighten up the screws" on our spiritual lives and to try harder to be more in control. For example, there are those who use Lent as a time to stop smoking or drinking. Some people in the past, and maybe even now, abstained within their marriages from sexual intercourse on the grounds that even licit coitus is dangerously close to uncontrolled lust.

In Charlotte Brontë's psychological romance *Jane Eyre,* Edward Rochester kept his demented wife hidden on the third floor of his house while he attempted to carry on a normal life. When the wife escaped and appeared downstairs, Rochester could only hide the reality behind a rigid exterior. Lent is a good time for acknowledging, in the company of our Lord, the "third floor" of our worlds. There is no possibility of wholeness until we do. Otherwise, with Rochester, we will continue to live with our shame and present a good face to the world. It is helpful to recall the history of Lent as a time in which the catechumens underwent exorcism. We cannot exorcise demons when we refuse to confess or even acknowledge their existence. It is well to remember in this season the words of the seventeenth-century Puritan divine, Richard Baxter, "Christ leads us through no darker rooms than he has gone before."

The First Sunday in Lent

Lutheran	Roman Catholic	Episcopal	Pres/UCC/Chr	Meth/COCU
Gen. 22:1–18	Gen. 9:8–15	Gen. 9:8–17	Gen. 9:8–15	Gen. 9:8–17
Rom. 8:31–39	1 Pet. 3:18–22	1 Pet. 3:18–22	1 Pet. 3:18–22	1 Pet. 3:18–22
Mark 1:12–15	Mark 1:12–15	Mark 1:9–13	Mark 1:12–15	Mark 1:9–15

EXEGESIS

First Lesson: Gen. 9:8–17. The text stems from the Priestly writer who begins the flood story by emphasizing that earth and humanity were full of violence and totally corrupt (6:11ff.). God therefore decides to destroy all human beings, except Noah and his family. Today's text represents the climactic end of this P story of God's punishment of humanity in the great flood, elaborating the promise and pledge of God never again to annihilate humanity as long as the earth exists.

Although the P writer shares with many ancient writers the notion that God can destroy or annihilate the world, the story must be seen in the context of a prophetic announcement of judgment and salvation, which is distinct from other ancient statements about the destructive power and intention of God. The P story focuses the threat mainly upon Israel, the people of God, and not so much upon outsiders. As the drama of God's judgment affects the people of Israel in particular, so the prophetic announcement of salvation is also spoken for and directed toward Israel. The primordial story of the flood must be seen in the context of this prophetic announcement of judgment and salvation—for the history of Israel and for the eschatological end time.

The major theological motif of this climactic section (9:8–17) is that of the covenant. The P writer underlines this motif by stating it over and over again (cf. vv. 9, 11, 12, 13, 15, 16, 17). In contrast to the covenants at Sinai and with Abraham, P makes no mention here of a mutual contract and commitment between God and humanity. The covenant is more God's pledge or promise never to turn from the decision not to destory the earth.

In addition to the spoken promise and pledge, God also gives the sign of the rainbow as assurance of the divine will and action for humanity's salvation. Some exegetes claim that the author saw the sign of the rainbow as the bow of a warrior, that is, God's weapon. By placing it in heaven, God makes it a sign that war and its violence are over. Other exegetes maintain that it is sufficient to see the rainbow as a sign of nature. After the chaos and storm of the Flood, it is seen to signify the divine light and salvation breaking through the clouds and destruction. In any case, the rainbow hanging high in heaven is not just a sign for the people of Israel. It is also a reminder of the promise God made never to destroy the earth (vv. 15ff.). The rainbow, therefore, is the sign of God's faithful remembrance of the promise made to Noah and his descendants. God's everlasting covenant and pledge are given to all of creation, all of history, and all of humanity.

Second Lesson: 1 Pet. 3:18–22. This is a rather difficult passage. Its selection is probably due to its allusion to the "days of Noah," who is mentioned in the First Lesson for today as well. Despite considerable exegetical discussion and analysis, this reference (as well as the whole of vv. 19–20) is rather obscure and should not be interpreted in light of the later understanding of Christ's descent into hell enunciated in the creed.

Exegetes are divided on both the formal delineation of the passage and its context in the history of religions. The wording and form of the passage show great affinity with the christological hymn in 1 Tim. 3:16. There is still considerable debate as to the degree of interdependence between them—whether, for example, 1 Tim. 3:16 is a condensation of 1 Pet. 3:18–22, or 1 Pet. 3:18–22 is an elaboration and expansion of the shorter form. It is also possible that both texts derive from a traditional hymn whose original form is no longer available to us.

Even more difficult to determine is the history-of-religions context for the mythological statement in vv. 19ff. It is likely that the Enoch story provides the mythological framework. First Enoch refers to the fallen angels of Gen. 6: 1–4 and reports that the patriarch Enoch was commissioned to go to them and talk with them (1 Enoch 12:4ff; 13:4–10). Moreover, in this tradition the punishment of the fallen angels is closely connected to the Flood (cf. Wisd. of Sol. 14:6). Second Pet. 4:2–4 makes an explicit connection between the punishment of the fallen angels and the saving of Noah in the Flood. The theological meaning of the mythological statement in 1 Pet. 3:19ff., then, would be that no one, not even one in Hades, is exempted from the salvific power of Christ and the gospel. This is underlined in 4:6 which stresses that the gospel is preached even to the dead.

It is difficult to give any definite interpretation to this passage because only v. 18 stands within the contextual argument of the letter. V. 18 gives meaning to the undeserved sufferings of Christians (vv. 13–17) by pointing to the undeserved suffering of the just Christ and to his resurrection as participation in the sphere of the Spirit. Christ the just died for us the unjust in order to bring us to God. This stress on the suffering of Christ refers back to 2:18—3:6 and points forward to 4:1ff.

This hymnic statement is followed by a series of soteriological statements: Christ's postmortal preaching to the "imprisoned spirits" (v. 19ff) is followed by an interlinking of water and salvation in the Flood story (v. 20) which in turn prepares for the notion of the salvific waters of baptism. The whole soteriological sequence culminates in a hymnic announcement of the resurrection and exaltation of Christ. Though only a few were saved from the flood, the salvific power of Christ extends to everyone in the whole cosmos, even to the fallen spirits and the dead. Baptism is not, therefore—as in Judaism and pagan religion—a purification rite, but it is a pledge and commitment (not appeal) to God. Baptism's saving effect is rooted in the resurrection of Christ. Whereas 2:21–25 and 4:1–6 stress the suffering and passion of Christ, the Christology of 3:18–22 is one of triumph and victory.

Gospel: Mark 1:9–15. The Gospel reading is part of the prologue to Mark's Gospel. The prologue begins with the preaching of John the Baptizer announcing Jesus' ministry (1:1–8), the baptism of Jesus, and his messianic endowment with the Spirit (1:9–11).

That Jesus was baptized by John is undoubtedly historically accurate, for the event would have raised too many problems for the primitive church to have later inserted it into the tradition. For example, v. 4 states that John preached a baptism of repentance for the forgiveness of sins, and we can see in Matthew's version of the story that there was early objection to the thought that Jesus needed baptism for such a reason (cf. Matt. 3:13–15).

Mark's emphasis in the baptism account lies elsewhere. First, traditions of the Isaianic corpus are called upon to proclaim that Jesus is the recipient of the Spirit from God. The heavens are rent (cf. Isa. 64:1) and Jesus sees, in a revelation given to him alone (so too in Matt. 3:16; cf. Luke 3:21–22), the Spirit descending upon him like a dove. The origin of the symbolism of the dove is unknown, but the objective nature of the gift is underlined. This is not just an inner experience on Jesus' part; the Spirit comes from outside of him, from God. Then a voice from heaven, obviously intended to be God's voice, makes two announcements: "Thou art my beloved Son," and "with thee I am well pleased." The latter is taken from Second Isaiah (42:1b) and reflects the gift of the Spirit to the suffering servant in that book.

Second, God's announcement of Jesus' sonship draws on the royal traditions of Israel (cf. 2 Sam. 7:14) and specifically quotes Ps. 2:7, which is a royal psalm connected with the coronation of a Davidic king.

Two announcements are therefore made about Jesus in the baptism account. He is the Davidic heir to the throne, the long-awaited Messiah or Anointed One who, according to Isa. 11:2, was to be given a sevenfold gift of the Spirit. But he is also the suffering servant promised by Second Isaiah, who too was to be anointed with the Spirit of God. Thus Jesus' messiahship and his suffering are linked from the very first in Mark's Gospel, and they are not to be separated.

The Spirit of God commissions Jesus to his royal and suffering office, but it also gives him the ability to fulfill it. The Spirit is understood here, and frequently elsewhere in the Bible, as enabling power. There is no thought that Jesus, as a human being, has divine power in himself. He is not to be worshiped for himself alone, nor are his mighty acts indications of his self-enclosed divinity. His ministry and his person are understandable only in their relation to God and the gift of God's Spirit. Jesus is Son to the Father, acting by God's power and fulfilling God's purpose of the kingdom. Thus, he comes announcing the advent of God's rule (1:15).

The fact that the announcement of Jesus' messiahship in the baptism is followed immediately by the temptation in the wilderness once again serves to emphasize that he is a suffering royal figure.

The temptation story (1:12–13) is closely linked both traditionally and structurally with the scene of Jesus' preaching and ministry (1:14–15). The Markan version of the temptation story is very short and concise when compared with that of Q in Matthew and Luke. The two accounts seem to present different traditions. While the logia source Q stresses Jesus' fasting during the forty days in the desert, Mark emphasizes his being nourished with heavenly food.

The temptation scene reflects motifs also found in Jewish apocryphal writings, especially the *Life of Adam and Eve*. This book claims that Satan was thrown out of heaven for refusing to adore Adam, the image of God. Satan then seduced Adam and Eve, with the result that they were banished from paradise where they had been nourished with angelic food. Their penance lasted forty days and, after their expulsion, they experienced the enmity of the wild animals.

In a similar fashion, Mark's temptation scene is dominated by paradise motifs. Jesus seems here to be imagined as the "new Adam." As Adam and Eve were tempted, so is Jesus. Yet unlike Adam and Eve, he does not succumb to the temptation of Satan. Therefore the wild animals consort with him, and the angels serve him heavenly food. Jesus the "new Adam" is, in a new manner, child and image of God. As God's especially "beloved one" he is filled with the Spirit who empowers him. Because Jesus has overcome Satan, the personification of evil and all demonic powers, he can inaugurate the new aeon and reign of God where Satan's power is broken. Although according to Mark the life of Jesus is full of trials and temptations, these are not satanic but human trials. Jesus' powers of exorcism restore the humanity of people and are a sign that Satan is overcome (1:21–28, 32–34, 39; 3:11, 22–30; 5:1–20; 9:14–29).

While the first part of the reading points to Jesus as inaugurator of a new humanity and world, the second part is a summary of Jesus' preaching of the gospel (1:14–15). After the execution of John, Jesus returns from Judea (1:5, 9) to Galilee, his native country and the center of his ministry. He proclaims the "gospel of God," an expression often found in pre-Markan and Pauline missionary traditions. The content of the "good news" consists in the announcement of salvation and in the call to repentance and faith in the gospel. The announcement of salvation is formulated as a prophetic-apocalyptic messenger-call stressing the verbal expressions "fulfilled," "has come near," and "is at hand," which are related in a synthetic parallelism interpreting each other. The time of God's salvific rule and power has arrived; God's dominion is impinging on this world.

Jesus invites his hearers to "repent," turn totally away from their old way of life, and recast everything. Not the threat of judgment, but the announcement of salvation invites *metanoia* "conversion." Such a conversion must be expressed in belief in the gospel. In the Markan redactional verse 1:1 the gospel seems to be identical with belief in Jesus, but here the content of the gospel is the announcement of the salvific reign of God. Therefore it is likely that this formulation reflects pre-Markan theology and probably the message of Jesus himself. In Jesus' ministry the "new world of God" is present initially: this life world of God is free of satanic-evil powers destructive of human life. As the "new creation," it spells peace with animals and nature as well as healing of illness and infirmities. Belief in the gospel means a reorientation of one's life towards this salvific power and world of God.

HOMILETICAL INTERPRETATION

First Lesson: Gen. 9:8–17. There is something profoundly moving about this account to which the exegesis points. The dates of the Priestly writers are in dispute, but certainly they flourished at a time when Israel was experiencing great hardship. A succession of empires—the Assyrian, the Chaldean, and the Persian—held the Israelites in a continuous bondage of varying degrees of severity. Amid this suffering the Priestly writers understood what had happened as a judgment upon the nation, but also as an embodiment of the promise of salvation.

The primordial story of the Flood, common to many Near Eastern cultures, became the setting for an eschatological promise. The sign of that covenant is the rainbow, the aftermath of rain—given as a promise of fertility to a people living on the margin of the desert under constant threat of drought and starvation. There is a graciousness in this gift associated with the beauty of nature that stands in pleasing contrast to the violence of humanity and the cruelty of nature.

If we take our Lenten discipline seriously and do more than satisfy ourselves with a trivial piety, we will inevitably encounter the violence and cruelty in which we are participants. There is hardly an experienced pastor who has not known persons who, because they had so little understanding of sin, in all honesty believed that they were not sinners. Their understanding extended no further than the ancient Christian quaternion of fornication, murder, theft, and apostasy.

This is a time to discover the radical judgment that falls upon us all who in countless ways do violence to God's vision for his creation. Sin is rebellion against God, the wrenching of life from its roots in the divine purpose. It can only lead to death. We all share in this, by sins of both commission and omission. We are partners in creating the burned-out inner cities, in generating the hatred spread by such groups as the Ku Klux Klan, in perpetuating the familial climate leading to chemical dependence, child abuse, and divorce, and in failing to be good stewards of the earth.

Joseph Conrad in *The Heart of Darkness* spoke of "the horror, the horror, the horror." The same feeling underlies the grim story of the Vietnam War recounted in the movie *Apocalypse Now*. It is the unblinking gaze into the human psyche that sees only the horror. It is the awareness of this horror that can lead a people to conceive of a God who, like ourselves, can annihilate what in love he has created.

This picture of the human condition is not overdrawn. When, in spite of this, God promises to be forever faithful and sets as the sign of his covenant a most beautiful phenomenon of nature, the contrast is startling. The contrast is what gives the gospel power. If we looked at ourselves through rose-colored glasses and, in the spirit of Emile Coue, convinced ourselves that "every day in every way I am getting better and better," then a God who loves us would not be such good news.

The only thing worse than Coueism is to call the evil good. The American novelist Ayn Rand taught an ethic of violent greed in which if God existed, he would be our adversary. We have to either embrace God's horror or fight horror with horror.

God is not to be lowered to the level of our own cruelty. He neither will destory us nor condone our sin. No matter how we may act, he is faithful to himself and persists as our constant lover. We may turn his earth into nuclear rubble, and yet he gives us the rainbow. This is the promise that evil shall not prevail over good or hatred over love, even if we crucify what is good and loving in the name of self-sufficiency, self-interest, or some other God of the misbegotten self.

Second Lesson: 1 Pet. 3:18–22. The difficulty of this passage depends a great deal upon the assumptions one makes in reading it. As the exegesis points out, the passage draws liberally upon the mythic heritage and liturgical life of the people to whom it is addressed (as in the hymn upon which both this passage and 1 Timothy 3:16 may well have depended). The author is developing in broad strokes a series of images that stimulate the imagination of his readers in order to give substance to his thesis that all the created order is subject to Christ's saving action.

This is entirely consistent with the OT lesson and is a good reason for both lessons to be read on the same Sunday. The God in the covenant of Noah loves without ceasing the people he has made. The God revealed in Christ seeks the salvation of all people, *even* the kind of people he drowned in the Flood described in the Noah story. If this be true, our present suffering becomes tolerable in the knowledge of God's love and fidelity.

This love and fidelity are particularly manifest in baptism. The sacraments are a window into the divine reality. They enable the participants to look on the world as God sees it and to be formed by that reality. The Greek word in v. 21, often translated "conscience" (*suneidēseōs*), has a root meaning of consciousness. The idea is that baptism is a coming-into-awareness. This is something of what Justin Martyr meant in the second century when he spoke of baptism as the illumination. This is a more positive notion of baptism and, consequently, of Christian discipleship than that of simply the removal of the stain of original sin.

If we see God as revealed in the Christ who is Lord of all, then it is possible for us to understand that he whom we serve is indeed Lord of lords and King of kings. All creation is subject to him, including those who have already died. The Christ in this passage is not only a Jewish eschatological prophet, he is the instrument of God's creative purpose to fulfill all things as he has planned: past, present, and future. What by virtue of our baptism we discover is that the Christ is a cosmic savior. His gospel is that God is faithful and God's love will prevail.

The typology drawn between the waters of the Flood and the waters of baptism is not altogether satisfying. The waters of the Red Sea in the Exodus story are more immediately obvious in relating the meaning of baptism, but Christianity has historically drawn on the waters of the Flood as well. Baptism has to do with drowning the evil self and then coming up on dry land as a new self. It is the promise that lies in baptism which is emphasized: God is loving and faithful.

There is probably no time in history when there is not an abundance of despair among the people. Certainly our time is no exception. Lent can be an occasion to reenforce our despair, which I would distinguish from our dread. Despair is like wandering through an empty desert, where there is no meaning or even a hope of meaning. Dread is like wandering through a jungle filled with things beautiful and terrifying, with the constant apprehension of being overwhelmed by all that meaning. What we need to do when in despair is move to dread: to open our inner eye and see all, both beautiful and terrifying, that abounds in our life. This is a step on the way to discovering that God is faithful and loving to all creation.

The reference to baptism and sacramental theology at this point is not incidental. The sacraments are what strengthen and guide the pilgrim in the jungle of many and diverse meanings. Karl Rahner, the German Jesuit theologian, described the "exhibitive meaning" of the sacraments. They call us into the "event" of salvation in the midst of our despair. That event is the love and fidelity of Christ, which flows from his Passion. Amid all the principalities and powers, symbols and diabols, promises and threats, Christ brings us by the power of his resurrection, in which we are incorporated in baptism, to a proleptic of our final union with God.

In some Orthodox churches the words over the main entrance read: "This is the gate of heaven." The point is that what goes on within that church is a foretaste of the heavenly banquet envisioned in the Revelation of John the Divine. This passage from 1 Peter draws upon that same anticipation by gathering up images indicative of the salvific power of the cosmic Christ. It is a vision of the worship life of the people of God worth preaching.

Gospel: Mark 1:9–15. A central theme in this passage is the desert or wilderness. The gift of the Spirit in his baptism by John not only proclaims to Jesus his messianic vocation, it drives him into the desert. Having known the desert, Jesus can return to preach the breaking-in of the kingdom of God and call others to repentance.

The people in the ancient world almost universally lived within walled cities. When Aristotle described human beings as "political creatures," he meant that by nature humanity lives in a *polis* (a walled city-state). He also said that outside the city one is either a god or a beast. This territory between cities is not governed by law but is a place outside the structures that guide our routine existence.

There is a possible analogy between the ancient idea of the desert or wilderness, the risky territory outside the city walls, and that wilderness that lies in our personal and corporate lives. It is essential if we are to live together without destroying each other that we be governed by law. Our own inner lives must be structured by predictable norms of conduct, or we would have no sense of self. But the structures exact a price. They blunt our awareness by appearing to define the world as it is, rather than serving as partial and fallible descriptions of conventional behavior.

This blunting of our vision is particularly the case in a secular culture such as our own. There is no expectation of God in our world. If we reflect on the treatment of life's crucial issues in our public media, the absence of transcendent value is obvious. Conventional wisdom today is overwhelmingly godless.

The experience of the Spirit always brings our conventional lives into question. God enters our life in a way that makes us newly aware of his presence and call. But if we respond, the first thing that happens is that we are driven into the wilderness, a world strangely without the familiar landmarks and the predictable patterns of living. In that wilderness lies the possibility of new life or of destruction. It is always a risk to come face-to-face with the living God. Mark speaks of wild beasts and angels. In the two-thousand-year tradition of Christian spirituality the beasts signify the temptations of our lower nature, which could devour us. The angels are, of course, the messengers of God. Beasts and angels live side by side.

It is a popular idea that if we know the Spirit and are converted life will be easier for us. On the contrary, the Spirit drives us into our own wilderness, where we have to wrestle with what pulls and tugs at our being. It has always been there, but we were previously unaware of it. Repentance (*metanoia*) means to see things in a new way. The blinders of conventional living are removed, and we perceive ourselves as we never have before. There is the offer of God's reign over our life, but there is also the temptation of a life of sin or rebellion against God.

What enables us to face the wilderness with hope is the gospel. Jesus not only came preaching repentance, the new vision of what lies beyond our inner and corporate conventions, but he also offered the gospel, the good news of God promising that we will come through the wilderness a new person. The challenge of the gospel is never "to play it safe," to hide in the security of nostalgia, the old patterns, the comfort of the familiar, or the assurance of our status. We are called out. There seems to be a certain congruence between the people of God as the *ecclesia* (those who have been "called out") and the Spirit driving Jesus out into the wilderness. We are a pilgrim people, who must travel by the light of the gospel through the territory between the cities in our quest of the heavenly city.

The Second Sunday in Lent

Lutheran	Roman Catholic	Episcopal	Pres/UCC/Chr	Meth/COCU
Gen. 28:10–17 (18–22)	Gen. 22:1–2, 9, 10–13, 15–18	Gen. 22:1–14	Gen. 22:1–2, 9–13	Gen. 28:10–22 or Gen. 22:1–18
Rom. 5:1–11	Rom. 8:31b–34	Rom. 8:31–39	Rom. 8:31–39	Rom. 8:31–39
Mark 8:31–38	Mark 9:2–10	Mark 8:31–38	Mark 9:1–9	Mark 8:31–38

EXEGESIS

First Lesson: Gen. 28:10–22. This first reading is part of the narrative of "Jacob's Dream at Bethel" which extends to v. 22. The present text combines strands of the Yahwistic and Elohistic sources. The names for God, Elohim and Yahweh, alternate with each other (cf. vv. 21–22 and 16–17). In the manner of the Yahwist, the Lord speaks directly with Jacob (v. 13); in the manner of the Elohist, God communicates with Jacob in a dream (v. 12). The repetition of the exclamations in vv. 16 and 17 also indicate separate sources. Formally, the whole narrative is best classified as an etiological cult legend that explains why the name Bethel (house of Elohim) replaces the older name of the town which was Luz. Historically, Bethel was an influential cult center until the seventh century when its cult site was destroyed by Josiah (2 Kings 23:15).

Theologically, the story highlights the deeper meaning of Jacob's sudden departure and flight from the murderous intentions of Esau (cf. 27:41–46). The God of Abraham and Isaac will become Jacob's God. Yahweh will protect Jacob and multiply his offspring and descendants. This theological assurance is present in a twofold way in the present form of the story. On the one hand, the dream of the stairway or ramp (not ladder) extending from heaven to earth is a sign of Yahweh's presence, which is added to God's direct promise. On the other hand, response to this experience confirms that this is the place of God's presence, and Jacob's vow underlines the promise of Yahweh.

The imagery of the dream refers to the Mesopotamian temple tower, the ziggurat. In ancient Babylonia and Assyria a pyramidal temple tower, with the appearance of a series of terraces or steps, rose beside the main temple, the so-called *Tieftempel.* This temple tower was thought to provide a summit point where one could visit and communicate with the godhead. The temple tower image, not that of the ladder, is used here. The imagery of the dream, therefore, suggests that Bethel is the place where communication with the heavenly world takes place.

God's presence means not only blessings but also protection and guidance for present and future generations. God is revealed here as a faithful God who will not fail to keep the promises he has made. Jacob's vow, in response to the experience of God's presence, repeats the motifs expressed in the speech of God. The protection of God will extend to the necessary means of survival: food, clothing, and safety. God's presence and protection should not be spiritualized. It expresses itself in everyday care for the necessities of survival both now and in the future. The cult at Bethel was instituted as an expression of gratitude for God's faithfulness and protection.

Second Lesson: Rom. 8:31–39. This passage is the climax, not merely of chapter 8, but of the whole section (Rom. 5–8). Throughout these chapters Paul has elaborated the foundations of both Christian existence and hope and the corresponding Christian behavior. V. 31 seems to sum up his argument: "If God is for us, who can be against us?" This statement also draws chapter 8 to a close. After having dealt with the Christian life in the spirit (vv. 1–11), Paul identifies the "new world of God" created by the power of the spirit in terms of "the glorious liberty of the children of God" (vv. 12–17). Then, in vv. 18–30, he elaborates the promise and hope that creation itself shall be liberated from its bondage to demonic powers and share in the glorious freedom of the children of God. The section climaxes with the statement that those are made just and glorious whom God has elected and called (v. 30).

Vv. 31–39 are formulated in the eloquent style of the Greco-Roman diatribe in which rhetorical questions and answers follow each other in rapid sequence. After the introductory question (v. 31a), the first exchange seems to follow in vv. 31–32. The second interchange is found in vv. 33–34, while the third is in vv. 35–39. But vv. 38–39 do not merely respond to the question in v. 35, they sum up the whole section. The key questions appear to be: first, "If God is on our side, who is against us?" second, "Who can bring charges against God's elect?" and third, "Who shall separate us from the love of Christ?" The entire passage, therefore, appears to revolve around the question of whether or not Christians, as "God's children," could ultimately fail to achieve full salvation.

The first question is met with the assertion that God has shown himself to be "the God for us" in the saving event of the death and resurrection of Christ. The expression "God gave him up for all" probably reflects a liturgical tradition, but it is not certain that Paul interprets this action of

God with reference to Abraham's sacrifice of his son (cf. Gen. 22: 16, LXX). The God who has given over to us the beloved son will not refuse anything to us.

The second question and response is expressed in forensic language. The construction of the argument is somewhat obscured because of the diatribe style. It is possible that there are two questions being asked: who can bring a charge?—God who justified; and who can condemn? —Christ who died. Or it is possible that only one question—who can bring a charge?—is being asked and receives two responses. In any case, the theological meaning of the interchange is clear. The answer is still "No one," especially since Christ not only died and was raised for us but is now also our intercessor (cf. v. 27 where the Spirit is the intercessor) before God.

The third exchange draws our focus from heaven to earth and elaborates "the God for us" in terms of "the Christ for us": "Who shall separate us from the love of Christ?" The elaboration of sufferings and persecutions encountered by Christians is not merely rhetorical but probably reflects their real situation. Some Christians might have doubted the "God for us" and the love of the Christ because they experienced tribulations and sufferings. Therefore, Paul refers them to the fate of Christ their Lord as well as to Scripture (Ps. 44:22).

Vv. 38–39 sum up Paul's entire argument by expressing his certainty that nothing and no one in heaven or on earth can separate Christians from the love of Christ, which he seems to envision here as a superpower separating us from the world and binding us irreversibly to the power of the "God for us." Sufferings, persecutions and death, far from disproving this, are the attestation that we belong to the "new world" of God.

Gospel: Mark 8:31–38. The introduction to the second part of Mark's Gospel (8:27—9:1) presents Jesus' open revelation to the disciples. While in the first part of the Gospel Jesus speaks in parables and signs, now he openly begins to teach his disciples about his own "way" to the cross and the demands of discipleship. In the preceding chapters, the disciples had failed to understand Jesus' mission and ministry and had remained unenlightened despite all the miraculous events (8:21) they had been privileged to experience. Now in this second section, their incomprehension deepens to misunderstanding.

The central section of the Gospel (8:27—10:52) is skillfully composed, using the motif of "the way." (8:27; 9:33f; 10:17; 10:32). This section is subdivided by three passion-resurrection predictions (8:31; 9:31;

10:33f.) which articulate the final goal and end of "this way": Jesus' journey will end in his passion and execution in Jerusalem. Each of these passion-resurrection predictions is followed by a conversation about discipleship. True discipleship is only possible by following Jesus on "his way" of suffering and service.

Mark does not disqualify the confession of Peter at Caesarea Philippi that Jesus is the Christ, the Messiah, the Anointed One, (8:27–30). Through the literary device of the so-called "messianic secret," he limits this christological confession to the time after the resurrection (8:30 cf. 9:9). Moreover, he interprets the confession of Jesus as the Christ through the first passion-resurrection announcement that is rejected by Peter. In response, Jesus rebukes Peter as a spokesman of Satan and not of God (8:33). This first passion-resurrection announcement is followed by a string of four discipleship sayings (8:34–37), which climax in an apocalyptic announcement of the future coming of the Human One (Son of Man) for judgment (8:38), together with a saying which refers to the future reign of God (9:1). Though the three passion predictions in Mark are clearly redactional, already before Mark, the announcement of the passion and suffering of Jesus must have been connected with the call to discipleship and with the saying about "saving one's real life." Both motifs are also combined in John 12:24–26, which presents a tradition different from that of the Synoptics.

The passage centers around the motif of suffering and discipleship. Jesus' messiahship must not be misunderstood. Jesus is not exempted from suffering and death. His disciples, therefore, should not dream of glory but must be prepared to follow him on the way to death. The image of discipleship presented here is the image of Jesus as one condemned as a criminal who takes up his cross and starts out on the way to his execution (cf. Luke 14:27). The painful way to his execution begins for Jesus here and now, and Peter's attempt to detract him from this preordained way must be rejected as satanic temptation.

The disciples must be prepared to surrender and risk their lives in following the crucified Messiah, even to death. The Markan community lives between the death and resurrection of Jesus on the one hand (8:31) and his Parousia on the other (8:38). In the meantime they must live lives of discipleship, prepared to suffer persecution and death. While this first discussion on true discipleship emphasizes that the disciple must follow Jesus on his way of persecution, the second and third discipleship discussions (9:33–37; 10:35–45) stress discipleship as servanthood and as taking the last place within the community. Jesus does not just preach "the way" but lives and shows it so that, in following Jesus on the way, the disciples will learn not only the true identity and meaning of the life of Jesus but also how to live as Christians.

The sayings on discipleship should not, therefore, be misunderstood as demands to suffer for suffering's sake or for self-denial as a way to ascetic perfection. Following Jesus means awareness that one's life can end as Jesus' did in violent persecution and death. Discipleship is totally oriented toward the "new humanity" and salvific power of God. Thus it radically throws into question all power gained by domination, subjugation, and the furthering of one's own interests in the place of service. The Markan community lives between the resurrection of Jesus and his eschatological return. As they follow Jesus "on the way" which he has shown them, they are not to deny him, even in the face of persecution, but they are to become instead a community of disciples characterized by a radical reversal of values and power relationships.

HOMILETICAL INTERPRETATION

First Lesson: Gen. 28:10–22. There is a responsive chord struck by the words, "Truly the Lord is in this place, and I did not know it." Jacob speaks for the well-intentioned, everyday believer, who is happy to say that he believes in God but whose faith possesses little immediacy. This new awareness of God's presence comes to Jacob when he is off guard; that is, Yahweh appears to him in a dream. Often the everyday believer is caught by surprise, not when he is looking for God but when he has retreated from the routine, secular world.

The image of what we traditionally translate "ladder," but which the exegesis points out is much more likely a Mesopotamian ziggurat is evocative. Throughout the Christian tradition, the ladder has been a sign of spiritual growth or ascent, but the symbol has its roots in pre-Christian, Near Eastern religions. Little ladders are found in Egyptian tombs, placed there to help the soul climb from the under world to the upper world. Numerous Christian writers have treated the subject; for example, the fourteenth-century English spiritual guide Walter Hilton, who wrote *The Scale* [*Ladder*] *of Perfection*.

In this passage Jacob does not ascend the ladder to God, as one might climb a ziggurat or ascend the steps of spiritual perfection, but Yahweh *comes to him* in the form of angels or messengers. The movement is toward humanity, which is a crucial insight for the Christian. Suddenly, the Lord himself is there. Angels are symbols pointing to the presence of God, who is always there. God is one who reveals himself. Our knowledge of him is not the result of our vigorous effort to unveil him, although we have to be receptive to God's disclosure of himself.

The result of this self-disclosure is a promise embedded in a mystery. Yahweh does not make everything right for Jacob. He has not arrived, by any stretch of the imagination, in the kingdom of the perfected. Rather, God promises to be a companion on the way, assuring Jacob that the way has a goal and direction. The land on which Jacob lies will be his and that of his descendants. He will live on in his people.

But just as important as the promise is the awe it provokes in Jacob. This feeling of Jacob's is a sense of the numinous, a questioning in the face of an awareness of his own dependence. The promise leaps out from the mystery. If life were one dimensional and only the present counted—the past being irretrievable and the future unknowable—then there could be no promise. But the question posed at the horizon of our knowing—Where did I come from and where am I going?—evokes the promise of God. This is what is meant by being receptive to God's self-disclosure.

Maria Rilke, the early twentieth-century Austrian poet, once wrote an aspiring young poet that he should love and live the questions. Alice Toklas asked Gertrude Stein as the latter was being wheeled into the operating room from which she never returned, "What are the answers?" Stein replied, "What are the questions?" God's answer is the promise, which comes as we have the courage to question the mystery of our own contingency. Edward Hays, a Roman Catholic spiritual director, has written that a truly great religion does not give answers so much as it raises great questions that challenge the believer to search inwardly for the answers. It is not the secularist who is brave when he says that life is meaningless; anyone can wring his hands in despair. It is not the theist who claims to have all the answers. It is the believer who pierces the darkness that surrounds us all with the question of faith.

The passage ends with Jacob bargaining with God. If God will be with him and provide all his needs, then he, Jacob, will serve and worship God. The tone of this passage slips dramatically. We discover that Jacob is like the rest of us. He sees his service of Yahweh more as a transaction than as an unconditional, mutual love. Such an attitude inevitably reflects a puerile faith and sets us up for disappointment. Human freedom requires a deeper relationship with God than a simple quid pro quo.

Second Lesson: Rom. 8:31–39. A seminary professor of mine once said that there are certain great texts on which one should not preach until one has been in the business twenty-five years. Whether or not this admonition should be followed, this passage is certainly one of the texts my professor had in mind.

The heart of this diatribe—the word in Greek means literally "to rub away"—is the confident declaration in v. 37 that "in spite of all, victory is ours through him who loved us." Paul is not going to leave us in our safe pessimism. He wears us down with the power of his argument. There is nothing small about the stage on which Paul perceives the cosmic drama being waged between the forces of evil and the forces of good. Every individual battle against sin is a microcosm of creation's struggle to be brought to fulfillment.

Obviously, there is much that works against us. Christians do not win popularity contests nor are they guaranteed material success. There is a certain irony in the contrast between Paul's description of the suffering of the church at Rome and the typical American presupposition that Christian commitment is evidenced by financial success—what Richard Hofstader called American "practical religion." The latter is more in the tradition of the Jewish wisdom literature than typical of experience of the early church. Paul believes that the greatest human need is not for worldly success but is derived from the fact that we are separated by our rebellion from the life-giving God. Even if in the eyes of the world we are failures, still we are not under judgment because God is the one justifying us through Christ's passion.

It is very easy to abuse that notion. It has been used as grounds for tyranny, self-righteousness, and laziness. Who are "all of us" for whom the Son of God was given up? Who are the "elect"? Clearly Paul meant at least the Christians in Rome. But it would be erroneous to assume that he was implying a theology of election, where Christ died for only some and not for all. This would be a contradiction of the spirit of his entire ministry. It is a message of hope for all who are oppressed and unwilling to settle for the bondage of the ordinary expectations of secular humanity.

The good news which Paul so eloquently proclaims is for all who recognize their oppression and discover in Christ the possibility of freedom from the bondage of boredom. In our age Christ is both law and salvation. He convicts us of sin by his witness to a more complete humanity but also offers us the way out of that slavery.

Most people never get as far as being convicted. They live a trivial existence. Their lives seem to be essentially an exercise in keeping themselves entertained. Is there anything for which we are willing to die? The possibility that there is nothing can be the most depressing realization of our times. Twenty years ago, Philip Rieff described contemporary humanity as "psychological man." He explained that we had "therapized" ourselves out of the obsession with issues and had found a way to live a life of contentment, free of emotional investment. It seemed in the turbulent sixties that he was wrong, but in this narcissistic age we have recaptured "psychological man."

The excitement of this passage with its promise of victory comes from the awareness that restlessness and struggle are characteristic of humanity at its best. The issue is one of eternal life or death. Gregory of Nyssa, a fourth-century spiritual writer, said, "Already at birth we are driven by the very nature of things toward our departure, for which we must carefully prepare." This is a high doctrine of humanity. It is to the driven nature of humanity that Paul addresses Romans 5–8 and to which he offers this concluding promise of ultimate victory.

At a clergy conference I once asked the rhetorical question: "What do you do with your time?" A voice from the rear answered: "Help people get through the night." How can we do this? Certainly not by pretending that night is really day. It would appear at times that some imply there is only night, which is hardly good news. Paul believes our night is real, but there is promise. "For I am convinced," he says, "that there is nothing . . . that can separate us from the love of God in Christ Jesus our Lord."

Gospel: Mark 8:31–38. The Christian understanding of the way to union with God stands in stark contrast to Jacob's bargaining with God about his following of the way. If one is a true disciple, he may not expect to be provided with his every material need. On the contrary, the faithful disciple may expect to suffer. After all, we serve a Lord who not only had to endure the cross, but who, in fact, followed a road which he knew led to the pain and death of Calvary.

Contemporary Christians often have trouble with suffering. Most of us recognize that seeking suffering for its own sake—perceiving the Christian life as an obstacle course whose successful completion guarantees perfection—is contrary to the gospel. But in reaction to this perversion we substitute one which is worse: the notion that the true believer is delivered from suffering. The gospel clearly teaches that, like Christ, we shall experience the cross if we are to be his disciples.

Peter's rebuke of Jesus is paradigmatic of the attitude which holds that he who accepts Jesus as Lord will experience prosperity (much as Jacob bargained with God). There is abroad the teaching that the Christian succeeds better in business, sport, and love because he is a Christian. This misses the depth of creation's brokenness and of the radical change that must be effected if God's vision for the world is to be realized. Such an attitude is as satanic now as it was on the lips of Peter.

The passage calls us to the imitation of Christ. This is a subtle vocation. It was in the twelfth century, principally in the teaching of Bernard of Clairvaux, that the church emphasized devotion to the humanity of Jesus and taught us to follow his example. Francis of Assisi in the next century introduced meditation upon the Passion of Christ and introduced such novelties as the visit to the Christmas crib. The impact of the imitation of Christ upon later medieval piety and the modern western church is incalculable. For example, the Pietism of the early eighteenth century, as exemplified in someone like Count von Zinzendorf, taught a devotion to Jesus which has profoundly shaped American religious devotion.

The great danger in the imitation of Christ is the temptation of a sentimental literalism to make Jesus a cultural hero or to romanticize the first century. Nikos Kazantzakis, the Greek novelist, described such sentimentality as being "smothered to death in lard." Actually, the expression "to take up your cross" pre-dates Christianity and was a way of stating the necessity to accept the burden of life, with all the suffering that inevitably ensues. It could be interpreted as a Stoic admonition to do one's duty for its own sake, a notion that creeps into Christian ethical teaching from time to time.

However, the subtle calling of the Christian disciple is neither to a cloying imitation of an ersatz messiah nor to simple endurance. Rather, the disciple accepts his cross and shares it with the Crucified One. In so doing, the disciple experiences in the midst of suffering the gift of new life. This is how God thinks, as contrasted with typical human thinking.

The reference to thinking—"You do not think the things of God but the things of men"—recalls Paul's admonition to the Philippians: "Think this among yourselves which also is in Christ Jesus" (2:5). The Greek word for "think" is the same in both instances. Thinking refers to the sense that we make of our world or how we perceive reality. The created world is a product of God's thinking. Our task as disciples is to be co-creators, sharing in God's thinking. As Paul puts it, our task is to think as Christ thinks, who is the incarnate presence of the mind of God.

The Christian disciple sees suffering as God sees it. It is a condition of human freedom. To avoid suffering at the price of our freedom is demonic. It destroys what God wishes for his creation. This avoidance is, consequently, radically sinful.

The Third Sunday in Lent

Lutheran	Roman Catholic	Episcopal	Pres/UCC/Chr	Meth/COCU
Exod. 20:1–17	Exod. 20:1–17 or Exod. 20:1–3, 7–8, 12–17	Exod. 20:1–17	Exod. 20:1–3, 7–8, 12–17	Exod. 20:1–17
1 Cor. 1:22–25	1 Cor. 1:22–25	Rom. 7:13–25	1 Cor. 1:22–25	1 Cor. 1:22–25
John 2:13–22	John 2:13–25	John 2:13–22	John 2:13–25	John 2:13–25

EXEGESIS

First Lesson: Exod. 20:1–17. Probably no other OT text has had more concrete influence on the life and ethics of Christians than the Ten Commandments. Yet, in the OT, they are never called commandments but are understood simply as the *Ten Words*. This indicates that the Decalogue was not so much perceived as law and regulations but as the revelation of the will of Israel's God. Therefore, rather than presenting ethical or legal norms, the Decalogue spells out what is absolutely abhorrent in the eyes of Yahweh.

The Decalogue is given in two forms—Exod. 20 and Deut. 5. Exod. 20 is generally attributed to the Elohist writer but, in its present form, is probably the product of many reformulations. Its negative apodictic form and its positive reformulations of the commandments concerning the Sabbath and parents indicate a process of reinterpretation; that is, the text had a past life before being cast in its present form. Whether or not the history of the tradition reaches back to Sinai and Moses is difficult to determine—and probably no longer possible. What is more important theologically, however, is the setting (*Sitz im Leben*) of the Decalogue tradition in the liturgical celebration of the covenant.

Critical investigations of form have shown that, during the period of the Judges and even later, the Decalogue was the climax of the festival at Shechem. Here, every seven years, they celebrated the renewal of the covenant (cf. Deut. 31:10f.). The liturgical sequence of this great festival was as follows: a parenetic introduction, a proclamation of the commandments and renewal of the covenant, and a conclusion of blessings and curses. Thus, the Decalogue was part of the commemoration and celebration of the revelation and covenant of Yahweh and was experienced by Israel at a given moment in history as a saving event. The cultic festival and pilgrimage to Shechem renewed and made present the saving event for each succeeding generation.

The Decalogue, therefore, should not be made absolute and taken out of its theological context, since it is exactly the context of the covenant of God with Israel which gives meaning to the Ten Words. Ancient understanding held that people who made a treaty and entered into a special relationship with a god were bound to accept specific ordinances as expressive of the relationship. It was Yahweh who liberated Israel from the bondage of Egypt and made Israel a special priestly people and holy nation. In the commandments Yahweh proclaims divine right and sovereignty over Israel. By accepting Yahweh's will for justice and righteousness, the people of Israel express their gratitude and loyalty to God.

This divine will pertains both to Israel's relationship to God and to Israel's relationships among its people. Yet, a wide area of everyday life is neither regulated nor circumscribed. Thus the Ten Words do not subject Israel to comprehensive, normative regulations but delineate appropriate behavior for certain marginal situations (idolatry, murder, violation of property). The goal of these ordinances is expressed in Deut. 4:6ff.: "They will say 'How wise and understanding is this people!' For where is there so great a nation to whom God is so near as Yahweh, our God, whenever we call upon God? And where is there so great a people that has statutes and ordinances so righteous . . ." The proper responses to the revelation of the Decalogue, then, are not feelings of guilt and legalistic scrupulosity, but the unconditional acceptance of Yahweh's salvific will for justice, as well as pride and thanksgiving.

Second Lesson: 1 Cor. 1:22–25. Paul has written the whole section, 1 Cor. 1:10—4:21, as an apologetic defense of his apostolic authority and leadership. Within this *apologia* the theme of wisdom plays a major role. Paul mentions wisdom first in the opening passage 1:17 and last in 3:19, a segment which deals with Paul's apostolic authority and influence within the Corinthian church. Paul's elaborate discussion of the wisdom topic, within the context of the defense of his leadership, indicates that this topic was of major concern to the Corinthians as well as to Paul. However, Paul's theology of wisdom (*sophia*) seems to differ from that of the Corinthian pneumatics, which Paul appears to correct and to modify. His discussion of this theology of *sophia* within the present context in 1 Cor. shows that for Paul the issue was not an abstract theological problem of definition but had far-reaching consequences and implications for Christian life, community, and leadership.

First Cor. 1:18–25 is an elaborate play on words and contrasting juxtapositions. It spells out a contrast between the Wisdom of God and the wisdom of the world, between wisdom and folly, and between power and weakness. The fundamental antithesis is between Divine Wisdom and human wisdom, the wisdom of the world and the word of the cross. Paul heightens this fundamental antithesis by employing the notion of reversal. He labels as foolish and weak what usually is considered wise and strong, while he claims the foolishness of the cross to be the Wisdom of God.

The meaning of the passage appears obvious. The Pauline contrast and reversal is often taken to be between intellectual knowledge, wisdom, and learning on the one hand and the uneducated foolishness and simplicity of the Christians on the other hand. Yet such an anti-intellectual interpretation is a complete misreading of the Pauline argument that should be understood from its historical-religious context. This context of Paul's argument is generally identified as either gnostic or Jewish-Hellenistic wisdom theology. Those assuming a gnostic context insist that, for Paul, *sophia* had no anthropological correlate, whereas the Corinthian pneumatics understood themselves to be united with the heavenly, transhistorical *Sophia*. They, therefore, saw themselves as privileged to leap over the mundane realities of historical existence. They believed the powers of heavenly wisdom were exhibited in tongues of angels, miracles, extraordinary signs, and ecstatic experiences.

However, this assumption that *sophia* has an anthropological reference for the Corinthian pneumatics but not for Paul is contradicted by the elaborate argument of 2:6–16. V. 1:24, which introduces Divine Wisdom as something that is preached, links section 1:18–25 with 2:6–16. The true *Sophia* of God is found only in Christ crucified. He is, according to 1:30, our righteousness, sanctification, and redemption. Thus it seems that Paul deliberately does not use the term *sophia* in the fundamental contrast 1:18ff. but takes it up in a negative sense in the contrasting use of v. 21a. He ends with a positive affirmation of this contrast in vv. 24f. and 30. The *sophia* of which Paul speaks is not the wisdom of this age or that of the powers of this world but the Divine *Sophia* and is identical with the crucified Christ. (cf. 2:6–8).

While the Corinthian pneumatics seem to have considered the passion and execution of Jesus as peripheral to their spiritual endowment with heavenly wisdom and their intimate communion with the Lord of glory, Paul insists that those who have received the spirit of God are able to perceive the mystery of the cross as the true Wisdom of God. While religious persons, Greeks and Jews alike, desire to experience divine power manifest in the world and, therefore, seek for *sophia*, Paul sees the Wisdom of God as experientially available only in the foolishness and weakness that is given with the cross. Salvation is not achieved through mystical union with the Divine Spirit and in the participation in ecstatic miraculous powers but in and through the proclamation of Christ crucified, the *Sophia* and Power of God.

Since for Paul the key of Christian faith is the belief in the identity of the heavenly Lord with the crucified Jesus of Nazareth, he can say that the Wisdom of God is folly for those who belong to this perishing age. Therefore, he disclaims for himself the persuasiveness and lofty words of human wisdom and of the worldly-wise. He insists that he has preached nothing but the cross of Christ, which reveals God's salvific plan and intent. Paul implies that he, just as the Corinthian pneumatics, is able to speak in esoteric fashion, to reveal divine mysteries, and to exhibit great miraculous powers. Yet he does not do so. If he reveled in such esoteric wisdom and individualistic mysticism, he would not proclaim Divine *Sophia* but preach the wisdom of this world. For Paul then, communion with Divine *Sophia* implies primarily not spiritual perfection and esoteric religious experience but living out one's life under the paradigm of the cross of Christ.

Gospel: John 2:13–25. Jesus' prophetic protest in the temple is narrated in all four Gospels. Despite differences in detail, the action is the same in all four accounts: Jesus drove merchants and money-changers out of the temple court. The basic difference between the Synoptic and Johannine accounts is one of timing. According to the Synoptics, the event took place shortly before Jesus' trial and execution; in John, the scene inaugurates Jesus' public ministry.

Connected with the story of the cleansing of the temple precincts is an interpretive saying (John 2:19) which the Synoptics put on the lips of false witnesses; in John, it is Jesus who says it and is then misunderstood. A similar saying is found in connection with the trial of Stephen in Acts 6:14. This saying, transmitted in a sixfold tradition, relegates the Jerusalem temple to the old aeon and predicts that it will be replaced by a new eschatological temple, which Mark interprets ecclesiologically and John christologically. The temple "not made with hands" is, for Mark, the Christian community; in the Fourth Gospel, it is the resurrected body of Christ.

The theological interests of the Fourth Evangelist are clear. From the very beginning of Jesus' public ministry, a deep gulf existed between Jesus and official Judaism, one which widens over the course of the narrative. The days before Passover were busy days for animal sellers and money-changers because the temple tax paid by every Israelite had to be paid in ancient Tyrian, rather than in Roman, coinage. With his prophetic action, Jesus severely incriminates such cultic business transactions as alien to the worship and house of God. The injunction "Do not turn my parent's house into a marketplace" is justified by his disciples with a Scriptural proof text (Ps. 69:9) which draws out the dangerous consequences for Jesus' fate—he will have to pay for this action with his life.

The interpretive temple saying is set within a dialogical challenge from the Jews. They ask for a sign, a prophetic miracle, something which would legitimize Jesus' action. A typical Johannine "misunderstanding" helps to clarify the saying about the destruction and building up of the temple. V. 22 stresses that it was only after Jesus' resurrection that his disciples understood his word and believed it. The body of the resurrected Lord is the true place for worshiping God. In similar fashion, Jesus' dialogue with the Samaritan woman (ch. 4) stresses that perfect eschatological worship is worship in "Spirit and Truth," thus abolishing all cultic institutional worship, even that of the Jerusalem temple. The possibility for this new way of worshiping God is opened up by Christ's death and resurrection.

Vv. 23–25 do not properly belong to the story of the cleansing of the temple but serve as a transition to the discourse with Nicodemus, who represents one of those many persons in Jerusalem who had come to believe in Jesus. The three verses probably come from the Evangelist himself and not from the so-called Signs Source. The writer has composed them to connect 2:13–22 and 3:1–21.

John alone among the gospel writers presents Jesus' miracles as signs which call forth faith, that is, as those acts which reveal Jesus' glory and therefore the fact that he has come from God. V. 23 does not say what deeds Jesus performed in Jerusalem, but they were obviously of a miraculous nature, comparable to the changing of the water into wine at Cana (2:1–11). There, too, Jesus' work called forth faith on the part of the disciples (2:11).

In this passage, however, such faith is seen as ambiguous. Signs can prompt genuine faith, as in 2:11, but they can also call forth the belief in Jesus as a mere wonderworker (cf. 4:48), a belief totally inadequate to Jesus' real nature as the Revealer of God (cf. 14:8–11). Certainly, faith based on signs is better than the hostility of the world, represented by the blindness and disbelief of the Jews in John. Yet, "blessed are those who have not seen and yet believe" (20:29).

Jesus does not trust himself to such frail trust on the part of the Jerusalem believers—the contrast between the two trusts is deliberate (v. 24). That is, Jesus has no confidence in their enthusiasm about him. He does not imagine they will be faithful followers or that their acclaim of him will turn aside the fate which his cleansing of the temple will bring upon him. The rejection of Jesus by "his own" (1:11) will come.

Jesus' refusal to accept the Jerusalem believers' faith as genuine is based, in vv. 24 and 25, on the fact that he knows human nature and is aware of what is in the human heart. Thus, John attributes to Jesus God's power to know our inmost thoughts (cf. Jer. 17:10; Ps. 139:1–4). Jesus and the Father are one. The Son shares in the Father's omniscience.

HOMILETICAL INTERPRETATION

First Lesson: Exod. 20:1–17. The Ten Commandments have for centuries been a source of proof texts for moralism. Moralism is the notion that there are certain ethical norms spoken by God and immediately and unequivocally placed upon humanity as an absolute demand. For moralism the Ten Commandments are self-evident and unambiguous, with no need for interpretation. There is no question of the historical context of the author or of the situation of the reader. Moralism does not understand the need for casuistry: it believes the will of God is self-evident. Moralism separates our private world from our public life.

The Ten Commandments have also been seen as an instrument in the moral education of the young. Church schools are admonished on occasion to teach young children the Ten Commandments in order that the children will "be good, knowing the difference between right and wrong." In this understanding information and formation are equivalent.

These two points of view fail to grasp the meaning of God, humanity, and sin. The Ten Commandments are a historical expression of a people who know God as one who calls us to justice and righteousness. They express the struggle of the Hebrews with the expectations of the God who led them out of Egypt to live their freedom in accordance with his will. The emphasis is upon a free people living under the sovereignty of God. Sin is the rebellion against the Lord who has a vision for his creation.

The Ten Commandments are not irrelevant to our time. Their meaning illumines our contemporary understanding of God's call among us. For example, the commandment to serve no other gods needs to be seen in a world where our other gods are no longer Baal, or Astarte, but scientism, materialism, or statism. The commandment to honor our father and mother is not a call to fulfill the obligations of the extended family in a patriarchial, agrarian society, but it has some very profound implications for living with our father and mother who are always a part of us. The admonition against adultery today exists neither for the purpose of protecting our property (that is, our wives) nor for guaranteeing our immortality in our children. It relates to a profound sense of mutual fidelity only recently identified in the Christian theology of marriage.

The God revealed in Christ, who is the God who spoke the Ten Words, calls us into a covenant that is not prescribed by laws written upon stone or in a book. He is the God, as Jeremiah tells us, who writes his covenant on our hearts. It is entirely right and appropriate to state ethical norms for our behavior, but they do not exist for their own ends. They are efforts to describe action which is most human, as God has made us to be human. They are a penultimate word. The ultimate word is the personal relationship between God and humanity. This is the covenant written upon our hearts.

Moral character is formed by living with people of moral character. It is a process of assimilation, not one of acquiring information. The Ten Commandments do not force our obedience; they measure the depth of our relationship with God and his people. They do this only after we have understood them in the light of two thousand years of Christian ethical teaching. As another example, most Christians are not committed to avoiding work on Saturday, which is the seventh day of the week, the Sabbath. There is a wholly different theological understanding embodied in our sanctification of Sunday, the first day of the week. The celebration of the resurrection on Sunday looks forward and consecrates what is to come. It is not principally a thanksgiving for what God has accomplished in the past. This only illustrates the care we must exercise in reflecting upon the Ten Commandments and making them our own.

Second Lesson: 1 Cor. 1:22–25. Those who use this passage to support an antiintellectualism in Christian discipleship could not be further from the point of the passage. In fact, that wisdom which enthusiasts often deride in the name of this passage is what Paul is advocating in opposition to the esoteric illumination of the Corinthian pneumatics. Preaching which interprets this passage needs to begin with the clear statement that for Paul, at least, wisdom is not something that comes from feeling good about Jesus or by denigrating learning. This is not a tirade against intellectuals, among whom Paul would certainly have to be included.

Recently, biblical scholars have recognized the profound influence of Jewish sapiential literature—for example, Job, Ecclesiastes, Ecclesiasticus, Wisdom—upon the authors of the New Testament and their understanding of Jesus. The concept of the Logos in the Fourth Gospel is now generally believed to be more characteristic of Wisdom literature than Stoic philosophy, although certainly there are mutual influences. Wisdom is neither esoteric knowledge nor information about someone or something. In the Wisdom of Solomon it is described as "intelligent and holy" (Wisd. 7:22), which is to say that he who is wise has discerned the divine plan.

Wisdom comes from what Richard of St. Victor, a twelfth-century spiritual writer living in Paris, called the contemplation of the "intelligibles." Contemplation is like the simple, fixed gaze of the lover, and the intelligibles are the inner meaning of a thing which is apprehended by a form of knowing quite different from the analytical approach of one who would feed all knowledge into a computer. This kind of knowing is like the understanding that arises from contemplating a great painting or listening to a musical masterpiece. It is what Michael Polanyi, an American philosopher of science, called "tacit knowing." Here knowing is participation—what is sometimes called "thinking with the left hand"—and the result is wisdom.

Paul tells us to think only of the crucified Lord, whom God has made his wisdom. In Christ upon the cross we have the manifestation of the mystery of God, which is God's hidden purpose. One has to apprehend the meaning of the Cross; it is not a knowledge we acquire by analysis. It demands a receptive form of knowing, a waiting upon God. It is both intelligent and holy, for it is the passion of the Wisdom of God.

This is hard for us to understand, because our culture usually perceives knowing to be a means of control. If one knows enough about something, then one can control it. If theology is an attempt to acquire power over humanity's relation with God and to do with it as one wills, it is not only justifiably condemned, it is a blasphemy. Some theologians behave as if they did control God. But what we need to remember is that authentic theology is at heart an act of prayer: a loving conversation between the finite mind of humankind and the infinite mind of God. This conversation aims at discovering, not imposing, an idea. Wisdom is gentle, like the twilight of a summer evening.

The crucifixion is an ordinary execution. Horrible, brutal, merciless, barbaric—crucifixion is all those things; but in the world of first century Rome, it was an ordinary form of repressing rebellion by a blunt object lesson, which could be observed regularly outside of countless provincial towns and cities. William Johnston, a Jesuit authority of the spiritual life teaching in Japan, is very much in the spirit of Paul when he says that "mysticism is a journey into the ordinary." The object of mysticism in Johnston's meaning—if I may redeem the word from its negative associations with the Corinthian pneumatics—is the Wisdom of God. When we look to the crucified Lord we take a journey into the ordinary and find there God's hidden, salvific plan.

Weakness and foolishness are not the same thing as stupidity. Popular piety and the cult of the common man teach that ignorance and holiness are directly related. This is to confuse piety with a lack of learning. A popular, very wealthy, western country music star remarked on television that what he hates most are the intellectuals. This kind of arrogance not only went unchallenged but the star proceeded to identify his followers with the weakness and foolishness of which Paul speaks. The weak and the foolish are more likely to be those who are oppressed by such arrogance and contempt in any form: intellectual, political, religious, or popular.

This passage is really about prayer, but it is also about hearing. Prayer begins with listening to what is proclaimed in the Passion of Christ. John of the Cross says that the word of God is the effect upon the soul. The word of God is power, because power is whatever can change us. Prayer is an attitude of being open to the power of God, his word, as manifest in the mystery of the Cross. To hear in this way is to discover the Wisdom of God.

Gospel: John 2:13–25. Cult is messy. If we are people who like things neatly defined, rationally explained, or carefully delineated, then good cult makes us uncomfortable. Cult is ritual, using the symbols of our religious faith to engage all our senses and to re-present for us those events which were enacted by the people of God. If those symbols are alive, they reach deeply within us and bring up to our consciousness all sorts of things both light and dark. Cult evokes, therefore, actions rooted in strong feelings; those actions are sometimes destructive and they are always dangerous.

All of this is seen in the presence of the money-changers and the merchants of sacrificial victims, who lived their greed; it is also seen in the cleansing of the temple by Jesus, who acted in righteous anger. If we are uncomfortable with these deep emotions then it helps us if we believe that the Christ is abolishing the cult. We can escape into the univocality of the religious concept. There is always a kind of prophetic docetism which wants to set the preaching of the Good News in opposition to its murkier solemnization.

One has to stretch the evidence beyond the breaking point to suggest that Jesus was advocating preaching as opposed to cult. Community, creed, and cult are integral qualities of all religion, including Judaism and Christianity. They are essential aspects of the formation of the disciple. The followers of the Christ, as well as Jesus himself, participated in the cult of their day; and many, apparently including Jesus, longed for the reform of the cult that it might better serve its God-given purpose.

There are two schools of thought: one sees the Fourth Gospel as eschatological in its meaning, and the other understands a sacramental theology to lie behind much of what the Evangelist says. In the second instance, it is interesting to speculate what John might have had in mind when he told us that the sign of Jesus' authority to cleanse our worship is his resurrected body; in 6:30ff., in response once more to a request for a sign, Jesus told his hearers that he was the living bread which if eaten, would enable them to share in his resurrection. Here is a new cult, a eucharistic cult, but not a docetic cult, as some may erroneously surmise from Jesus' words to the Samaritan women about worshiping "in spirit and truth." The Greek word in 6:51 for "eat" is like the German word *fressen*. It means to "gnaw" as an animal gnaws. It is not the language of someone spiritualizing worship.

Edward Schillebeecks, a contemporary Dutch Roman Catholic theologian, has suggested that the central experience of the resurrected Lord is that of forgiveness. The authentic cult, one in which we worship in relation to a belief in the risen Christ and in which we find life in feeding upon his resurrected body, is a means of coming into an awareness of forgiveness. The shackles of our sins are removed, not because we have followed the minutiae of the Jewish law that the money-changers and the sellers of pigeons served, but because Christ has given us our freedom. In worship we are formed by that freedom. We become Christ's disciples, we participate in the truth, and we are free.

Therefore it is helpful to contrast the prescriptive nature of the worship which gave rise to the temple abuses and the cult of his body to which Jesus calls us. In this passage, the Evangelist reminds us how easily human hearts are led astray, and this is no less true in liturgy than anywhere else. We make liturgy an end in itself, as do those who invest their lives in either changing it or in making sure it remains the same. A solemn conclave of the Russian Orthodox Church during the Russian Revolution debated the proper use of yellow in vestments. We have done things equally as insensitive. The freedom that comes from forgiveness opens us to a new awareness.

A sign can be understood as the substitute for awareness. If we have a proof of God's presence, we do not have to repent. We do not have to see the world in a different, more threatening manner. But the Christian cult, when it is true to its Lord, is not a sign but is the source of just such a deepened awareness.

The Fourth Sunday in Lent

Lutheran	Roman Catholic	Episcopal	Pres/UCC/Chr	Meth/COCU
Num. 21:4–9	2 Chron. 36: 14–17, 19–23	2 Chron. 36: 14–23	2 Chron. 36: 14–21	2 Chron. 36: 14–23
Eph. 2:4–10	Eph. 2:4–10	Eph. 2:4–10	Eph. 2:1–10	Eph. 2:1–10
John 3:14–21	John 3:14–21	John 6:4–15	John 3:14–21	John 3:14–21

EXEGESIS

First Lesson: Num. 21:4–9. This is one of those rare OT passages which refer to a cultic image. The Second Commandment prohibits the representation of Yahweh in the image of another God (Exod. 20:4–6), while the older form of the Decalogue (Deut. 27:15) forbids the making of an image of Yahweh at all. In making the "golden calf" (Exod. 32), Israel had transgressed this prohibition and the newly established covenant relationship with Yahweh had received a severe blow. True, Yahweh did not abandon Israel totally, but the people were punished by forty years in the wilderness, during which time the whole generation of those who had rebelled had to die (Num. 14:33–35). After the second departure from Kadesh (Num. 21:1f), Israel found itself once more at the Red Sea and from there advanced slowly to the Promised Land.

The present text, which can be attributed to the Elohistic writer, portrays Israel journeying through the desert (cf. also Deut. 8:15f.), plagued by hunger and thirst, and afraid of perishing in the wilderness. Once more, in their impatience, the people rebel and murmur against God and Moses. They are severely punished with snakebites, which kill many people. Israel repents, confesses its failure, and asks Moses to intercede with Yahweh to take away the snakes.

To remedy the calamity, Yahweh commands that Israel make an image of a serpent and mount it on a high pole where everyone can see it. The story presupposes a magic understanding: by looking at the image of the brazen serpent, someone bitten by it can be healed. The strange character of this ending is illumined by 2 Kings 18:4, where this episode accounts for an idol in the Jerusalem temple. King Hezekiah destroys the hill shrines, sacred pillars and sacred poles. He even demolishes the bronze serpent made by Moses, because the Israelites had been offering burnt sacrifices to it. But while 2 Kings is clearly aware of the idolatrous character of the bronze serpent image, the Numbers story seems not to be critical of it. In the ancient Near East the serpent symbol appears continually with the goddess in connection with prophecy, divine revelation and healing. The image of the bronze serpent becomes here a symbol for Yahweh's power for healing and forgiveness. According to 2 Kings 18:4, it was worshiped in the Jerusalem temple for seven hundred years.

Second Lesson: Eph. 2:4–10. While the syntactic-grammatical structure of this section is difficult, its topical-thematic outline is clear. The first section describes the time when the Ephesian Christians were still subject to Death's destructive power (vv. 1–3); the second elaborates God's life-renewing activity on behalf of the Christian community (vv. 4–7); and the third speaks of the final salvation of Christians in and through faith and grace (vv. 8–10). Whereas 1:20ff. had extolled God's saving activity with respect to Christ, this section deals with the community's salvation. The passage is determined by the opposition of past and present: their past life is "dead"; their present life—which as Christians they entered at baptism—is the real and true life.

As in the genuine Pauline letters, death is present here as an evil power. However, Ephesians sees death not so much in terms of a physical destructive power but as a spiritual power. Death expressed its destructive power in the former life of Christians through their desires and the instinctual promptings of their mortal human nature. As distinct from its perception by Paul, the power of the flesh in Ephesians seems actualized in anthropological terms. The influence and coercion of evil powers in this world can be detected in the former behavior of the Ephesian Christians.

God's mercy and love, however, have decisively changed this situation. The genuine Pauline letters do not speak of God's mercy, but later NT writings (cf. 1 Pet. 1:3; Titus 3:5) do so in the context of baptism. The love of God has been mentioned already (1:4ff.) in connection with our election and adoption as children by God, while 5:2, 25 speak of the love of Christ for the Christian community. As God has raised Christ from the dead and made him alive again (cf. 1:20), so God's mercy and love have taken Christians out of the realm of death and transferred them to the sphere of divine life and glory. God has brought them to life and saved them through their initiation into the Christian community. Whereas Paul is very careful to stress the future aspects of Christian salvation and glory (cf. Rom 6:1ff.), Ephesians emphasizes the finality of God's saving activity in Christ as a past event. Christians participate already, in and through baptism, in the resurrection and reign of Christ. Their glory, which is hidden now, will be revealed in the future. Thus Ephesians seems to abandon the "eschatological reservation" so carefully delineated in Pauline theology.

Vv. 8–10 develop and enhance the motif of v. 5. The new life, freed from the powers of death, is a gift of God's grace received through faith. Grace circumscribes the whole event of salvation. Whereas in Galatians and Romans the expression "through faith" has polemical overtones, this is not the case in Ephesians. The contrast to "works" here is not faith but "grace," not righteousness but salvation. Moreover, the "works" in this passage refer not to the Torah specifically but to human works generally. No human endeavor can achieve salvation.

Salvation is expressed here as "God's handiwork," that is, it describes the same reality as the Pauline expression "new creation" (cf. Gal. 6:15; 2 Cor. 5:17). Salvation—becoming a new humanity, a new creation—is given in and through Jesus Christ. The last sentence notes the goal of God's salvific work in Christ. We have become a new creation in order to become active in a life-praxis of "good works." The salvific activity of God must become manifest in history in and through our own lifesaving praxis. The realized eschatology in Ephesians remains oriented toward practice.

Gospel: John 3:14–21. These verses are not a part of the Gospel story and its action but a kerygmatic exposition by the Evangelist. They probably originated as an independently conceived summary and reflection on the message of Jesus. This theological reflection probably was incorporated into the Gospel narrative by disciples of the Evangelist during the Gospel's final state of redaction.

This meditation gathers together key motifs of Johannine theology. It speaks about revelation and the revealer, God's sending of Jesus, faith and judgment, light and darkness, evildoers and those who live by the truth. Jesus the Human Being is the revealer because his native home is heaven. The revealer has divine authority because he is sent by God. The witness and revelation of Jesus have public character because the whole world (cf. 3:17) is the realm into which he is sent. God's revelation in Jesus Christ is not a private religious event, not something which happens only in the individual soul, but something which happens before, and for, the whole world for the sake of the salvation of the cosmos. The reference to the bronze serpent, which in Wisd. of Sol. 16:6 is a symbol of salvation, expands the understanding of revelation to include salvation. Jesus' return to heaven begins with his exaltation on the cross where Jesus' power of salvation is disclosed (cf. also 12:32). Salvation is understood as eternal life and is offered to everyone who believes (3:15).

Jesus' death and resurrection—his exaltation—are the basis for the statements in vv. 16–18 which characterize the revelatory event in Jesus Christ as an act of divine love for the salvation of the world. The purpose of sending Jesus Christ is love and salvation, not judgment and eternal destruction. In sending the heavenly revealer, God wills the salvation, the well-being, of all humanity not just that of a privileged few.

Vv. 3:18–21 elaborate the possibilities opened up by God and the people's response to God's salvific initiative. These reflections arise from the historical experience of the Johannine community—namely, that not everyone responds with faith to God's gracious offer in Jesus Christ. Many choose darkness over light, judgment over salvation. Yet if this refusal to believe in God's revealer results in judgment, the outcome is not the result of God's intention but is, in fact, the person's own responsibility. People choose darkness over light, damnation over salvation, because their whole life-praxis is evil. Yet despite the historical experience of rejection of Christian faith and revelation, our theological meditation ends on a positive note. All who accept God's design for life and salvation by making Jesus Christ the truth of their life live in the divine realm and publicly manifest their life-practice as a sharing in the life of God. As Jesus is the revelation of the God who loves the world, so Christians in their life-praxis reveal God as a God of life and salvation.

HOMILETICAL INTERPRETATION

First Lesson: Num. 21:4–9. The imaginal possibilities of this passage when taken with the Gospel are fascinating. In this discussion I will first discuss some possible meanings of the serpent and, in the exposition of the Gospel, I will expand on this in terms of the role of Christ.

In the history of religion and in psychology serpents symbolize the coincidence and possible subsequent union of opposites. They are generally associated with female deities and, some psychologists believe, with the feminine in our own unconscious. Feminine consciousness, according to this theory, is particularly sensitive to ambivalence in human intentions. Female deities, for example, are often depicted as both nurturing and destructive and are therefore conceived of as capricious (for example, Inanna, who was the Sumerian goddess of love and war); but sometimes a nurturing goddess (for example, Demeter) will be balanced by a more penumbral female deity (for example, Kore).

The symbol of the Blessed Virgin Mary gathers about it these serpentine qualities. She is the "godbearer," the one who gives birth to the Messiah. But she is also the Madonna of the Pietà, who holds the dead Christ on her lap. We rejoice to see in her every woman who, like Dante's Beatrice, conveys an intimation of God's presence. But it is to Mary that we plead, "Pray for us now and at the hour of our death." There is a profound ambivalence in this contrast.

Think of the ambivalent position of the Israelites wandering in the desert and living the spartan existence of the nomad. They were free, but they were not free. Their Egyptian masters had been replaced by the cruelty of the wilderness. A tyranny they could identify was now replaced with the tyranny of the unknown. The first Christians, who believed that their Lord was raised and yet who had to live under the ignominy of serving one who was executed as a common criminal, must have experienced a common ambivalence. They were bitten by the serpents of ambivalence. Deep within themselves, as individuals and as a people, they had to struggle with conflicting wishes and values. Like the rest of us, at the very heart of their existence, the Israelites and the Christians were torn.

Asclepius was the ancient Greek god of healing. His symbol was the serpent. If a person wished to be healed, he went to the temple of the god and spent the night there. During the night the serpent would come and whisper in his ear what he needed to do to be healed. We are all familiar with the symbol of Asclepius, his staff entwined with two serpents.

In this view, healing was a restoration of harmony. This thinking is based upon a pathological theory rooted in the excess of one of the four humors. The opposites that war within us are united, so that they may work together to lead us to our true purpose. Health of body, mind, and spirit are, of course, intimately related, as is taught today in holistic medicine. It is no wonder that the author of the Wisdom of Solomon, a man obviously influenced by Greek ways of thinking, described the serpents in this passage as symbols of salvation—that is, the restoration of harmony and balance within the person.

It is significant that the healing comes after a recognition of the opposition within us. The serpent is a direct challenge to the cry for peace at any price. We must look upon the brazen serpent. Calvary is no accident on the way to the empty tomb. We have to explore the dark corners of our lives, intrapersonally, and interpersonally. There needs to be an acknowledgement of our sin, our incomplete being. We have been bitten by poisonous snakes, and we have very mixed emotions in following Christ.

The Gospel reminds us that we cannot serve two masters—God and mammon—at the same time. *The Shepherd of Hermas,* a second-century Christian writing, says our greatest failing as disciples is that we are double-minded or, literally, double-souled. The Beatitudes tell us that if we would see God, we must be pure in heart, which is the opposite of serving two masters or being double-minded. God heals our double-mindedness, our ambivalence. He helps us choose whom we will serve with singleness of heart.

Second Lesson: Eph. 2:4–10. This is perhaps the most succinct and moving testimony to God's free gift of grace in the NT. It is significant both for what it does say and for what it does *not* say. The notion of salvation by grace is a theological commonplace in the Christian tradition (not just beginning with Luther), and, as in all such cases, it is important that we keep some distance from frequently assumed interpretations.

In this passage the author is addressing the people of God, not individuals within the congregation. The NT really does not speak of individual salvation but of the resurrection of the community of the baptized. We are united with God much as we experience union in the Eucharist. The messianic banquet is an image that lurks in the background of Christian expectations.

Grace is not a commodity acquired at the price of our faith. The emphasis is all upon the freely offered presence of God, for this is what grace is—God present to us in power. The one mention of faith in v. 7—"For you have been saved by grace through faith"—carries the implication that faith describes our openness to God. Faith is the eye of love through which we enter into any intimate relationship. Faith is an attitude of trust, not something we do.

The quality of faith renders the Christian disciple vulnerable—one who is open to grace cannot be closed to God, his creation, or his people. God is present throughout his creation. There can be no selective attention to grace. This omnipresent nature of grace goes in the face of some claims to have faith. Such claims seem to set the faithful person apart from others. With such claims, there is little spirit of that risk which accompanies true vulnerability. There is a posturing in our Christian witness that falls short of any example of the faith of Christ, who embraced the sinners. The impression in this passage is that faith is a leap into the abyss of our uncertainty.

In this passage notice why God gives himself freely to us. It is not so that we may be freed from our sins or achieve our true end but in order that he may expend his wealth. The image is of an incalculably rich man, who, out of the superfluity of his love, puts on a stupendous party. God wants to display his immense resources and his superlative kindness in giving us his Son. It is like a father who gives his daughter, just out of love, as fine a wedding as he can.

This Dionysian quality in God's purposes is a great relief to the frequent interpretations of salvation by grace through faith. Too frequently it is interpreted legalistically in a strange desire to make God's grace commensurate with the degree of faith—as if God cared! We would be better off thinking of God's behavior here in terms of the returning prodigal son for whom the father kills the fatted calf. It is time for a party.

Good works are evidence, of course, for that relationship which God establishes through his grace. In our new life with God in Christ, we become privy to God's vision for the world. The author is no Quietist—a heresy particularly popular in the seventeenth century, which taught that the person united to God accepts passively God's will for him. We are expected to be persons of action, serving as God's co-creators.

A favorite word in the Pauline tradition is the Greek verb meaning to "walk about," as in v. 10. The verb carries the sense of being on the way. The way is marked with good works. There can be no separation of the Christian life from Christian action. God gives us a gift of his presence, but we respond by exhibiting our grasp of his vision for the world.

Gospel: John 3:14–21. The Evangelist or his redactors picked up the image of the brazen serpent from the Jewish tradition and used it to highlight the meaning of Jesus' crucifixion. The verb, which appears in v. 14, in Greek means "to be lifted up" and is ambivalent in its connotation. It can mean to lift up on the cross, that is, to crucify someone, or it can mean to lift someone up as to exalt, that is, to enthrone. The ambivalence of the Christian meaning of the cross is thus given form.

However, whereas the Hebrews were told to look upon the brazen serpent, the Christians are told to have faith in the crucified Lord. Gregory of Nyssa once wrote, "The chief act of faith in the 'mystery' is to look to him who suffered the passion for us." The act of faith is a way of seeing. Faith, as said before, is the eye of love. It pierces beneath the appearances to the reality of the object of faith. Faith is an attitude of participation in the other. Involved here is the same distinction as made by the late nineteenth-century English Jesuit poet Gerard Manley Hopkins when he distinguished between looking at a landscape and seeing the "inscape," the inner reality of the object of our attention.

Whoever sees the crucified Lord for who he is does not die, the Evangelist tells us, but comes into possession of eternal life. This is the healing which Christ brings. To be saved is to be healed. The Hebrew word, when translated into the Greek "to be saved," literally means "to give room to someone." There is no sense of God pronouncing judgment carried in this word. Our judgment is our own ambivalence as we are torn between the good we would do but cannot and the evil we would not do and yet do (Rom. 7:21–24). Within the space that God provides in Christ, his healing love can do its work.

Someone once put a bumper sticker on the car belonging to the OT professor at the seminary where I serve, saying, "Read the Bible. It will scare hell out of you." We do not need to read the Bible to be scared. Most of us are scared-to-death much of the time. We suspect that the darkness presses in on every side. We feel judged. Many people do a good job of appearing unjudged; but the chemical dependency, the inability to enter into any painful situation, the superficiality of most relationships, and the spirit of narcissistic self-indulgence common today should make us suspicious of that endemic cultural sociopathy which considers guilt merely evidence of neurosis.

The Bible gives a message of light to us who are in darkness. The Evangelist wrote that we love the darkness because it hides our evil deeds. It is easy to miss the point. The darkness hides our evil not so much from others as from ourselves. We suspect that we are evil. We narrow our world so that it becomes controllable, and the evil that operates lies outside of our consciousness. We plead ignorance of the millions that are starving, the suffering of minorities in the inner cities, the oppression of sexism, and the captivity of the corporate rich. Christ lightens our darkness but does not leave it an open sore. He heals it.

Some who profess Christ are like those with a persistent headache who are afraid to find out what is the cause because they fear it may be a brain tumor. They try everything but a medical examination. The crucified Lord proclaims that in the very worst situation, the senseless death of an innocent man as a common criminal, there is victory. We possess that victory when we incorporate the reality of the cross in our lives: the confrontation with evil and death—ours, society's, and the world's.

The Fifth Sunday in Lent

Lutheran	Roman Catholic	Episcopal	Pres/UCC/Chr	Meth/COCU
Jer. 31:31–34	Jer. 31:31–34	Jer. 31:31–34	Jer. 31:31–34	Jer. 31:31–34
Heb. 5:7–9	Heb. 5:7–9	Heb. 5:(1–4)	Heb. 5:7–10	Heb. 5:7–10
John 12:20–33	John 12:20–33	John 12:20–33	John 12:20–33	John 12:20–33

EXEGESIS

First Lesson: Jer. 31:31–34. This passage has become so familiar that its original power of vision can be lost. In order to recapture its hope and eschatological vision, we have to situate it within the context of the whole of Jeremiah. Throughout the book (cf. 7:23–28; 11:8ff.; 16:10–12; 25:3ff.; 35:14ff.; 44:4ff.) we hear the accusation that Israel has not listened to God's words and has not kept the covenant—ever since its entrance into the promised land (cf. 2:2ff.), through all the days of Jeremiah and up to the time of the collection and redaction of his prophetic words after the catastrophe. Although God took pains to keep the covenant with Israel, Israel "paid no heed and persisted in disobedience with evil and stubborn hearts" (7:24ff.). Jeremiah, therefore, announces a judgment which includes the whole history of Israel. Israel's total inability to listen and accept correction becomes the very starting point for Jeremiah's promise of the New Covenant.

The content of the New Covenant and those participating in it are the same as in the old covenant. Yahweh's self-revelation, Israel's election as God's special people, and the announcement of God's will for justice laid down in the Torah all remain. The difference between the Sinai Covenant and the New Covenant lies not in content but in process. Whereas, according to the Elohist, Israel could not endure God's direct address at Sinai and begged Moses to mediate the revelation of God's will to them (Exod. 20:18f.), the New Covenant requires no such mediation. Whereas the Torah of the Sinai Covenant was written on stone tablets, the New Covenant will be written into the hearts, the very being, of God's people. God will bypass the whole process of speaking and listening, of giving regulations and heeding them, of confronting human will with divine "other" will. What will change is not the covenant or the Torah or God but the innermost being of the people of Israel. As the result of the total internalization of the covenant and its obligations, all external teaching will become unnecessary. Why? Because all members will "know" (that is, will have communion with) God, and their sins will be forgiven, regardless of their high or low social status.

When Jeremiah speaks of the New Covenant, then, he has in mind Israel's final and total return to God. The people of Israel cannot, by themselves, straighten out their relationship to God anymore than Ethiopians can change their skin or leopards remove their spots (13:23). God has to create a new human self because the human heart is deceitful, incurable and obstinate. Just like the "nations," Israel is "uncircumcized in the heart" (cf. 4:4). While Israel transgresses the covenant day in and day out, Yahweh "does justice and right upon the earth, for on these I have set my heart" (9:24). The interpretive words of the Last Supper (1 Cor. 11:25; Luke 22:20) announce that the New Covenant, promised by Jeremiah, was initiated by the death of Jesus.

Second Lesson: Heb. 5:7–10. The immediate context of this passage speaks about the qualifications and election of the high priest (5:1–10). Because high priests are the representatives of their people before God, they are selected from the community in order to sacrifice for the atonement of the people's sins. Because of their own fallibility, high priests can be patient with those who are ignorant and full of error. Thus, high priests are instituted in their office not by virtue of their own achievements but by the election and call of God.

As this was the case with Aaron, so also was it the case with Christ who, in the words of Psalms 2:7 and 110, is characterized as the only adopted child of God, appointed high priest according to the order of

Melchizedek (5:1–6). According to Hebrews, Jesus is like Melchizedek—that is, Jesus being immortal is a priest forever and is therefore not like the Levites and Aaronites who were beset with human frailty and weakness (cf. ch. 7). A system of *taxis,* or status, is used to denote one's class or place in the hierarchical order which ranges from God down through creation. The closest kinship one can have with God is to belong to the *taxis* of children of God.

Vv. 5:5–9 are formulated within the world view of, and yet in contrast to, the Jewish-Hellenistic theology found, for example, in Philo, in which one must leave behind the world of the body—sensuality, flesh, blood, senses and passions—in order to move near to God and achieve "perfection." The imperfection of the world, seen in opposition to the divine reality, is experienced profoundly. Within this Jewish-Hellenistic tradition in which suffering is an education (*paideia*) which leads to progress, betterment and finally perfection, Jesus is the perfect heavenly being who has left behind the world of flesh and blood, suffering and imperfection. Trials and sufferings educate, edify, and exemplify piety and virtue.

According to vv. 7–9, Jesus has undergone this educative process in the realm of imperfection—he has been human, suffered and died. Jesus has achieved salvation and perfection for himself through prayer, obedience, outcries and sufferings. Therefore, he has ascended to the realm of perfection, heaven, where as the perfected child of God he is the high priest like Melchizedek. By this process, he has opened up salvation, that is, the way to perfection, for frail human beings still caught up in this world of passion. Contrary to Philo, Christians do not have to become supermen and superwomen in order to attain salvation. Rather, they can achieve perfection in faith and hope.

According to Hebrews' reinterpretation of this Jewish-Hellenistic theology, it is precisely in the realm of human imperfection and frailty that salvation is wrought. In Jesus Christ, God has reclaimed creation with its weaknesses, temptations, and human frailty. In his process of education to perfection, Christ has not left the world of imperfection behind but serves in heaven as high priest, merciful and sympathetic to the human condition of temptation and suffering. Whereas in the tradition of Greek *paideia* adopted in Philo or 4 Macc. the educational process of suffering leads to a state of religious perfection in which the pious leave behind sympathy, pathos, and mutual love, Hebrews insists that Christ—even in his perfection—continues to bind himself to the human realm of imperfection through sympathy, love, and "pathos" for his sisters and brothers on earth.

Gospel: John 12:20–33. The scene with the Greeks makes it clear that the Fourth Evangelist is writing from a retrospective viewpoint. The Greeks, probably proselytes, seek an appointment with Jesus through the disciples. The complicated protocol they had to observe in order to meet Jesus is elaborately described, but no direct response is given by Jesus to their request. The deeper meaning of the scene, however, is made clear when we see the statement of the Pharisees in v. 19 that "the world runs after him."

The access of the Hellenistic world to Jesus is achieved through his disciples, because it is only after Jesus' death and resurrection that the Gentile mission becomes possible. As the seed of corn must die in order to produce manifold fruit, so it is necessary for Jesus to die and to be exalted in order to draw all people to him (v. 32). The exaltation and glorification of Jesus is not a mythological event concerning Jesus only but an event of salvation for all of humanity. Jesus' death and glorification are the presupposition of the worldwide Christian mission. V. 24, therefore, can be understood as an indirect answer to the request of the Hellenistic world (the Greeks). Whereas the mission of Jesus of Nazareth had been confined to the Jews, through Jesus' death and resurrection the exalted Lord becomes accessible to the Gentile world as well.

At this point (vv. 25–26), two dominical sayings are introduced which, in their synoptic setting, follow the opposite sequence. The first saying stresses that life is of such a peculiar character as to elude any desire to have it at our disposal. Life is lost precisely when we cling to it and won when we are prepared to give it up. While v. 25 could refer to the life and death of Jesus, its connection with v. 26 makes clear its application to the life of the disciples. The Fourth Gospel thus interprets the dominical saying about discipleship differently than do the Synoptics. Instead of answering the Synoptic question Who is my real disciple? the sayings answer the question Who will follow Jesus and participate in his heavenly glory? The answer is clear: those who are servants of Jesus (*diakonos*). Jesus' promise that the servant will be wherever Jesus is, is ambiguous because it can mean participation in the suffering and death of Jesus as well as in his glorification. It is a promise which anticipates the promises made in the farewell discourses: those who follow Jesus will share in his glorification, and God will "love them."

Thus, if we read vv. 20–26 as a unified composition, the following answer to the Greeks' request is given. Access to the exalted Lord is possible only after Easter and only through service which leads to the acceptance of death. The exalted Jesus is not directly accessible in visions, miracles, or ecstasies but only by way of service and death.

This answer is underlined by the verses which follow, verses which are reminiscent of Jesus' agony in Gethsemane. Yet, more than any of the Synoptics, the Fourth Evangelist wants to make clear that the disturbance and trouble of Jesus have nothing to do with uncertainty or doubt about the outcome of the passion. Jesus is here, in control, and in charge all the way through. A divine voice interprets the obedience and submission of Jesus. Jesus' death manifests God's glory. Since the crowd cannot understand what is happening, the Evangelist takes this occasion to clarify the fact that eschatological judgment of the world is about to take place and that the evil power and ruler of this world is about to be cast out. When Jesus is "lifted up," that is, crucified and exalted, the time of the universal mission has come. Death brings forth life. The victory over the adversary of God becomes a missionary possibility of universal fruitfulness and salvation.

HOMILETICAL INTERPRETATION

First Lesson: Jer. 31–34. Jeremiah is struggling with a problem that has continually beset humanity's relation with God. There is something deeply satisfying in the notion that God is one who sets before us an external measure by which we must live. An Ugandan pastor, speaking of the suffering of his people following the overthrow of Idi Amin, explained that they understood this affliction as the punishment of God for their failure to abide by his law. Unmerited suffering was not something that he or they could comprehend because it raised questions about a God who has everything in his control, yet has made living in a chaotic world like Uganda unbearable.

There are many Americans today who, like their Ugandan brothers and sisters, find satisfaction in placing an objective law or set of ethical and cultural norms between themselves and God. God is seen in terms of certain moral and behavioral expectations that he has laid upon us. Whatever happens in our lives is understood as a consequence of our having fulfilled or failed to fulfill the divine will.

It is difficult for us to grasp how sharply this common understanding of God contrasts with Jeremiah's call for internalization of the covenant. Albert Mollegen, an Episcopal theologian and teacher, once told of an occasion when he was supplying in a parish on three successive Sundays. On the first Sunday he preached a sermon based upon the Covenant of Mt. Sinai in which he pounded home living by divine commandment. The congregation was most enthusiastic. The next Sunday he preached a Greek sermon on truth and beauty, and while the enthusiasm was more tempered it was still there. On the third Sunday he preached on grace and the inner life of the Christian. It was obvious that his hearers were unimpressed.

The words of this passage are familiar, but often we do not understand their implications. Our relationship to God is not in the nature of a transaction: If you do this, I will do that. Bargaining is out. God is not known by teaching *about* him. What he says, we are to do. God is as intimate to us as our innermost fantasy and our most deeply felt fears. The knowledge of God arises from reflection upon our internal life: the whisper of our conscience, the delight in the mysterious, and the fascination of surprise.

Christian behavior, if we take Jeremiah seriously, is not a matter of a sterile act of duty. It is the obedience to love. The Pharisees did their duty superbly. Jesus laid down his life out of love. Jesus did not come to destroy the Law but to give it life. The difference is the origin of our motivation. Sterile duty derives from a desire to *appear* righteous: the "unrighteous thoughts and feelings" are pressed within by the sacred response. The obedience to love, however, is a spontaneous movement of the transformed person from within to the world.

The important thing for us to realize is the difference between a God who lays down commandments to be followed and one who writes his law upon our hearts. This difference is related to the distinction between divination and revelation. Divination, the attempt by use of the occult to discover hidden knowledge, seeks to identify and control evil. Those for whom the knowledge of God is a matter of a rigidly followed external law are in some ways practicing divination. Revelation, the unveiling of the person of God, is the disclosure of the good and its incorporation into our lives.

Too much Christian practice is a subtle form of divination. I live in a community which is very self-conscious about being "Christian." When things do not go perfectly, when there is tension and strife, there is the inevitable request that we meet to find out what is wrong. The implication is that once the wrong is discovered, then it can be protected against, if not rooted out. This desire to find out the source of evil is accompanied by an intense anger, as if the presence of wrong were a personal affront to our own good intentions.

Good and evil are not external matters. Living with others requires that we look beyond the wrongs that separate us to the possibility of Christ in the other. It is what my sister or brother can tell me about the nature of God that should draw us closer. Short of the kingdom, there will never be a time when we do not hurt one another, but we are not called to keep score. What is expected is that we look upon the heart in order that we may see God's love written in living words.

Second Lesson: Heb. 5:7–10. Suffering is not something which God brings upon us or we seek out; it is what happens to us. Karl Marx not only said that religion is the opiate of the people but, in a much less quoted statement, remarked that religion is the "sigh of the oppressed." We are *all* oppressed by the human condition. At the very least, this means that we all must die, which is to say that we all must suffer. It is not a question of explaining the source of suffering. It is a question of living beyond the threat of ultimately being without meaning.

This passage speaks of the perfection of Jesus which he attained by obedience learned from suffering. The author explains that Christ becomes the cause of eternal salvation—a way of speaking of perfection, completion, or wholeness—to those who are obedient as he was obedient. Suffering is a discipline. It shapes us in the sense that it educates us, as the exegesis points out. Obedience is the commitment to that discipline.

These are strange words for our times. Contemporary Americans often think that suffering is something to be avoided at all costs, even the cost of our souls. We delude ourselves by thinking that we save ourselves by avoiding suffering. The classic example is our notion of a "successful marriage." When the suffering comes, which is only to be expected if marriage is a sign of Christ's fidelity and love as the NT teaches, we often seek a divorce. The reason given is that the pain of the marriage is destroying us. This passage would suggest that the hope for our personal wholeness lies not in escape from the painful but in obedience to the discipline of that suffering.

This is a heavy message and is not very likely to fall easily upon contemporary ears. But then our era is not unlike NT times. The Roman satirist Martial declared that all that interested his fellow citizens was "bread and circuses." We need only translate that to "tranquilizers and football."

It is interesting to raise the question of the doctrine of the atonement in this passage. As the exegesis points out, the author of Hebrews draws heavily upon the Greek notion of *paideia,* a theory of human growth that for centuries strongly influenced Christian *ascesis*. Christ is the classical hero whom we are to follow rather than a vicarious price paid to Satan.

The eastern or Persian contrast between light and darkness, the kingdom of God and the kingdom of Satan, is absent. What we find here is the Hellenistic notion of incompleteness seeking wholeness.

But not only is Christ the heroic example to be obeyed, he is the cause—the Greek word is *aitios*, from which we get "etiology," the study of causation—of our wholeness or perfection. We need to note that "perfection" does not pertain to our doing, but to our being. It is not a moral issue but a personal issue. Christ has established forever the way for the obedient to follow to union with God. The love of God expressed in Christ meets our human longing, and we are drawn up into eternal life.

This approach accords with Jeremiah's understanding of the law written upon the hearts of humanity. It is not a matter of an external transaction. The author of Hebrews does not suggest a forensic notion of the atonement. But neither is this simple exemplarism, that is, a Pelagian following of Jesus' example. The Hellenistic idea of *paideia* involved the transformation of the person, not just the external acquisition of information. It was formation in Christ. Jesus is the source of eternal life for those who are obedient to the discipline of the cross, because by this means he transforms our hearts and minds.

This idea of formation in Christ corresponds to Paul's notion that the Christian is to possess the mind of Christ. The essence of the person is the mind, and by being educated in Christ we think as Christ. This is a different notion of the salvific process than as either a forensic atonement or an external model to be followed.

Gospel: John 12:20–33. There is an often-told story of the young pastor who came to his first cure and preached what he had learned in seminary. Finally after months of inflicting his seminary notes on the congregation, he came to the pulpit and found a note on the desk. "Sir," it read, "we wish to see Jesus." In truth, there are pulpit desks that have these words carved into them as admonition to the would-be preacher.

But this story and the words addressed to the preacher can easily deceive us. The seeing of Jesus is not a simple matter. There is no immediate access to the Christ. Our Lord did not rise up and greet the Greeks who came seeking him. Instead he responded in that elliptical language so characteristic of the Fourth Evangelist. His divine mission is hidden. Jesus is seen in the act of service, even to the death.

There is a notion abroad that the Gospel is simple. If it is preached in its purity, people will flock to Jesus. It is hard to figure out this attitude. Certainly it did not have that effect upon those who heard Jesus himself preach. Many trailed after him asking for some proof of who he was, and when the nature of his mission was revealed upon Calvary only his mother and one lone disciple were left to watch through the final hours. Why do we think it would be any different now?

The word "glory" means the veiled-yet-evident presence of God. For the Fourth Evangelist our Lord's crucifixion is an act of glory. The presence and power of God are present yet hidden behind the suffering Jesus. To die upon the cross is Jesus' service to humankind. There our Lord God is to be seen for who he is in order that we all may be drawn to him. There is nothing simple in the realization that in the horror of a cruel execution—the agony, the blood, the barbarity, and the death—there is divine love. He who thinks it is simple has never seen such suffering. Jürgen Moltmann, a contemporary German theologian, has described Martin Luther's emblem of the cross entwined with roses. Such a cross, Moltmann tells us, contradicts the gospel and its understanding of the glory that is revealed. Christ died as painful a death as the cruelty of humanity has ever conceived for the punishment of its own.

In 1373—twenty-five years after a third to a half of the population of England had been wiped out by the plague and when the sick and harried Edward III of England was losing armies, land, and money in vast amounts to King Charles of France—Dame Julian of Norwich had a series of visions of the crucified Lord. It was this suffering Christ, so congruent with the pain of the English people, who said to Julian, "Sin is necessary, but all will be well, and all will be well, and every kind of thing will be well." This is no simple, optimistic gospel, but a perception of the glory that is revealed on Calvary.

In the Fourth Gospel, unlike in Hebrews, there is a cosmic struggle between the forces of light and darkness. The primordial principle of the world of darkness is banished by the power of the cross. It is not a real battle as we know who will win, because for this Evangelist, God is in control of the situation all along. For this reason and from our perspective, the Evangelist does not do justice to the nature of the mystery of Christ's love. To us God does not always appear to be in control. The power of the gospel is in direct proportion to the legitimacy of our fear that the darkness may in fact prevail.

Whether we understand ourselves as alienated and incomplete or simply in the dark, the fact that Jesus is there with us in every sense is what makes for the glory. Contrary to what would appear logical, we do not always stand on this side of the resurrection. It is not very helpful to remind people who feel anything but resurrected that they, like the Fourth Evangelist, must always possess a post-Easter mentality. This only evokes guilt. For people who cannot see Jesus, it is helpful to remind them that Jesus does not show himself off. Rather he holds before us the mystery of his Passion and calls for us to follow.

During the battle of Stalingrad, Helmut Thielicke preached to a German congregation whose sons, fathers, and husbands were dying on the outskirts of that city. He preached on the silence of God. His message was based on the text in which a Cannanite woman comes to Jesus telling him of a daughter tormented by a devil. You may recall that Jesus said not a word in reply (Matthew 15:22). God does not always respond with an answer to our questions and petitions. We may want to see Jesus as a savior, but sometimes the best we can hope for is to see him as a fellow slave.